THE SUCCESSFUL NEW MANAGER

The WorkSmart Series

The Basics of Business Writing
Commonsense Time Management
Effective Employee Orientation
Essentials of Total Quality Management
Goal Setting
Greater Customer Service on the Telephone
How to Become a Skillful Interviewer
How to Recognize & Reward Employees
How to Speak and Listen Effectively
The Power of Self-Esteem
Productive Performance Appraisals
Resolving Conflicts on the Job
The Successful New Manager
Successful Team Building

THE
SUCCESSFUL
NEW
MANAGER

Joseph T. Straub

amacom
AMERICAN MANAGEMENT ASSOCIATION
THE WORKSMART SERIES

New York • Atlanta • Boston • Chicago • Kansas City • San Francisco • Washington, D.C.
Brussels • Mexico City • Tokyo • Toronto

Library of Congress Cataloging-in-Publication Data

Straub, Joseph T.
    The successful new manager / Joseph T. Straub.
        p.   cm.
    ISBN 0-8144-7834-4
    1. Management.   I. Title.
HD31.S69656   1994
658.4—dc20   94-18779
                                              CIP

Printing number

10   9   8   7   6   5   4   3   2   1

For my wife,
Pat,
and our daughter,
Stacey,
with all my love

CONTENTS

PREFACE

It has been said that good luck happens when preparation meets opportunity. As a manager, you have an opportunity to build a satisfying and rewarding career. But what about preparation? That's where *The Successful New Manager* comes in. This is a down-to-earth, practical manual to help you understand and carry out some of the most basic and important tasks and functions that managers do and to cultivate skills that enable you to govern your future with confidence.

As you read and then work through the Review-and-Reflect activities at the end of each chapter, you'll convert this book into a highly personalized and valuable guide to mastering the many responsibilities and challenges that face you as a manager. When you're finished, you'll have created a customized desktop reference that's uniquely tailored to the nature of your employees, your job, and yourself. The Review-and-Reflect sections contain a variety of learning experiences:

- How Do You Rate? has you rate yourself according to key issues, techniques, or practices discussed in the chapter.
- True/False, Multiple Choice, and Matching exercises promote and test your understanding of major chapter concepts.
- Put It in Focus relates information in the chapter to your job, organization, and employees.
- What's Next? asks you to list specific actions you can take to improve your performance in the light of chapter discussion and your answers to other end-of-chapter exercises.
- Brainstormer's Corner provides opportunities to conceive activities to improve your efficiency, effective-

ness, and overall job performance based on the concepts and suggestions you learned about in the
chapter.

Your journey through *The Successful New Manager* will be
filled with self-analysis and self-discovery. By the time you
complete the last chapter, you'll possess insights, self-knowl-
edge, and a perspective that will serve as a solid foundation
on which to build a successful and rewarding future in
management.

CHAPTER 1

NEEDED: A NEW PERSPECTIVE

Becoming a manager is exciting and challenging—and perhaps a bit unsettling too. Although you've dreamed about and worked toward it for a long time, knowing that you've reached a higher rung on your personal success ladder naturally brings a touch of anxiety.

PLAYING A NEW ROLE

It's a big step up to the management level, and your new role may feel strange at first. Keep in mind, though, that culture shock hits everybody the first time they're promoted into supervision. People grow by being challenged, and every manager has felt the way you do now, thought many of the same thoughts, and shared many of the same concerns.

Somebody believed in you at least as much as you believe in yourself. So rest assured that you didn't get where you are today by accident.

There's more good news, too. Someone believed you were qualified to handle this job. Someone had enough confidence in your judgment to grant you this opportunity to stretch your wings and reach beyond your former responsibilities. Somebody believed in you at least as much as you believe in yourself. So rest assured that you didn't get where you are today by accident. You were most likely rewarded for the self-motivation, performance, and determination you displayed as a major contributor to the success of your organization.

So while you're thinking about your new responsibilities and the changes you'll experience in the days and weeks to come, remember to celebrate the likely fact that you've

1

earned this new opportunity. If that weren't true, you wouldn't have it.

CHANGING YOUR VIEWPOINT

You'll be challenged not only to feel comfortable in your new role but also to alter your point of view toward your work and your organization. More specifically, as a new manager, you must train yourself to:

- Define and solve problems and approach opportunities from management's side of the desk.
- Broaden your perspective to see the big picture as it's projected and relayed from above.
- Balance feelings of loyalty toward your subordinates with loyalty to your supervisors—a responsibility that comes with the territory of management no matter what level you're on.

COMMUNICATING UP THE LADDER

Before you entered management, you may have worried mostly about understanding your boss's directives and carrying them out to the best of your ability. Now you must become a pipeline for communication that flows both up and down. Your staff will expect you to relay their ideas, concerns, and problems to managers above you, to represent them clearly and fairly, and generally to "be a good boss" (which each of your employees may define differently—but more on that later). You must also communicate information from your level that helps managers above you plan, organize, direct, and control the activities of all the departments within the organization.

As a supervisor, you must also acknowledge, relay, and implement the goals and plans of managers above you through the people who work for you. This means you must reconcile demands and expectations that may conflict or operate at cross-purposes. This, too, is part and parcel of every manager's job.

MANAGING FORMER PEERS

The odds are that several coworkers were up for your promotion, but you walked away with the prize. Don't be surprised if they express jealousy or resentment. The same qualities that earned you your new job should serve you well here, however. Insulate yourself against petty complaints, backbiting, or gripes from colleagues who were passed over. Be objective, be fair, and be focused on making the most of your new career opportunity and confirming higher management's opinion that you were indeed the right candidate for the job.

In addition to deflecting former peers' resentment, you must resist their attempts to manipulate you, compromise your performance standards, or otherwise bend the rules "for old time's sake." You'll be challenged to be fair but firm and do what's best for the entire organization and for the management team of which you're now a part. This doesn't mean you should become aloof or withdrawn or appear to let your promotion go to your head. It does mean, however, that you're no longer "one of the guys."

COPING WITH STRANGERS

If you're supervising people you haven't worked with before, talk to them—and, more important, *listen* to them—about the nature of their jobs, the overall state of your department, and their special concerns.

Listening doesn't cost; it pays. Managers who ask for advice or opinions demonstrate wisdom by admitting they don't have all the answers. Moreover, your staff will be more willing to overlook your mistakes if you give them a fair audience and respect their opinions from day one.

Consider meeting members of a new group on their own

The best things and best people rise out of their separateness. I'm against a homogenized society because I want the cream to rise.

—ROBERT FROST

turf. They'll speak more candidly and comfortably than if they were summoned to your desk or cubicle. Sound out their feelings about work problems, suggestions for improvements, and opinions about such matters as work layout, equipment, training, and other issues that you may need to deal with once you're settled into your job.

You may want to review your employees' personnel files before you meet them to get a sense of their backgrounds, experience, previous assignments, and special skills. You'll also learn personal data that may help you establish rapport with them more easily.

Above all, reserve judgment on a new group of employees until after you've seen them from several sides and worked with them for several weeks.

USING FORMER BOSSES AS GUIDES

Invest some time evaluating and reflecting on traits that helped your previous bosses succeed and those that may have held them back. This may produce one of the best lists of do's and don'ts you'll ever find. Ask yourself questions such as these:

- How well did they communicate with others? What specific things did they do when giving instructions, listening, asking and answering questions, disciplining, announcing bad news, following up, and so on that worked especially well (or not so well)?
- How did they handle crises and react to bad news?
- Which bosses were exceptionally good at motivating subordinates? What did they do that made them excel?
- Which former managers were especially savvy about managing their time? What principles and practices did they use to help them?
- What record-keeping techniques did they use that you can adapt to your new job?
- How did your more successful bosses handle employee grievances and morale problems? What can you learn from your experience with them?

- What specific measures did they take to develop themselves and their staff? Which of these measures can you apply?

This isn't to imply, of course, that you should make yourself a clone or a composite of the best bosses you've had. Just the contrary is true. You bring your own unique personality, viewpoint, background, and experience to your new job, and given enough time and effort, you may become an even more effective manager than the best supervisor you've ever had.

Be prepared to employ your own methods, test your own ideas, and leave your unique mark on your job and the organization. In addition, appreciate the fact that there's no best way to supervise people. Changing management styles, employee diversity, and new trends and developments in management thought combine to make you a pioneer of sorts. Your former supervisors may not have had the benefit of the tools, skills, talents, and information that you have access to.

What qualities do people respect most in a supervisor? That question has no concise answer. One management professor and business writer asked hundreds of employees about the qualities they respected most in a boss, and here are two dozen answers that he heard most often. Use them as a hip-pocket guide to help you succeed. (Disregard the columns to the right of the list for now; you'll refer to them on your second reading.)

QUALITIES MOST RESPECTED IN SUPERVISORS

	Yes	No	Needs to Improve
1. Keeps us up-to-date on situations that affect future projects.	———	———	———

(continues)

	Yes	No	Needs to Improve
2. Maintains a positive attitude.	_____	_____	_____
3. Has sound oral and written communication skills.	_____	_____	_____
4. Explains actions and decisions that affect employees.	_____	_____	_____
5. Doesn't play favorites.	_____	_____	_____
6. Delegates authority and allows employees to do some of his or her job.	_____	_____	_____
7. Is specific when giving instructions about assignments.	_____	_____	_____
8. Gives employees incentives to improve their job knowledge and efficiency.	_____	_____	_____
9. Cross-trains employees so they can cover each other's absences.	_____	_____	_____
10. Gives praise for work well done; compliments as well as criticizes.	_____	_____	_____
11. Is aware of problems that employees are having with each other.	_____	_____	_____
12. Asks questions frequently; is a concerned and active listener.	_____	_____	_____
13. Organizes work schedules and assignments as effectively as possible.	_____	_____	_____
14. Displays a professional attitude toward the work and employees.	_____	_____	_____
15. Shows a human side; isn't compelled to act "the boss" all the time.	_____	_____	_____
16. Works with lower-level employees occasionally to understand what they do.	_____	_____	_____

	Yes	No	Needs to Improve
17. Takes time to listen to new ideas.	_____	_____	_____
18. Pays attention to broader problems; avoids nit-picking about details.	_____	_____	_____
19. Keeps others informed about changes.	_____	_____	_____
20. Discusses problems with subordinates as soon as possible instead of letting things reach a boiling point.	_____	_____	_____
21. Expresses feelings honestly.	_____	_____	_____
22. Attempts to know each employee as an individual.	_____	_____	_____
23. Uses new strategies that will make the organization more productive and competitive.	_____	_____	_____
24. Shows confidence in subordinates.	_____	_____	_____

REVIEW AND REFLECT

How Do You Rate?

Review each of the qualities of a good boss in the list just above, and rate yourself according to Yes (you have this quality), No (you lack this quality at the present time), or Needs to Improve (you have this quality but should take steps to improve it).

What's Next?

Review your answers to How Do You Rate? Then list specific, tangible actions you can take, *starting tomorrow*, to raise your rating on qualities you either lack or need to improve.

ACTIONS TO TAKE

_____

_____

_____

_____

_____

_____

_____

_____

_____

_____

_____

_____

_____

_____

_____

_____

_____

_____

_____

_____

_____

_____

CHAPTER 2

MANAGING YOUR TIME

Many new
managers
get bogged
down in
paperwork
and ignore
their
staff—or
spend so
much time
with their
staff that
they let
paperwork
slide.

Managing time effectively helps prevent or at least minimize many problems and distractions that would otherwise interrupt your work. This chapter describes time management techniques that you should apply from the start in your new job.

ORGANIZING PAPERWORK

Many new managers get bogged down in paperwork and ignore their staff—or spend so much time with their staff that they let paperwork slide.

One of your first tasks, then, is to develop ground rules for handling the blizzard of paperwork that crosses your desk:

• Set guidelines for sorting, prioritizing, and answering mail.

• Handle each document only once if possible.

• Don't let correspondence stack up. Robert Townsend, author of *Up the Organization* and the manager who made Avis one of the world's most successful auto-rental companies, liked to read his mail while standing next to a wastebasket, so he could discard unimportant items easily. If something needed a reply, he wrote his answer on the original, made a copy for his files (only if absolutely necessary), and returned it to the sender. Townsend claimed he could answer several dozen letters during a morning with this approach.

• Write standard or boilerplate formats, phrases, and

paragraphs that you can use in routine memos, letters, and reports. The time you invest to develop this uniform correspondence will pay off impressively later. Instead of writing the same replies over and over again, call up these prefabricated items on your personal computer (or retrieve them from a hard-copy file) whenever you need them.

• Make charts, time lines, or other visual aids to track and display the deadlines and status of reports, projects, and rush jobs.

• Categorize the regular correspondence you send and receive, and create a file folder for each category. Resist creating a miscellaneous file; it can grow into a monster. If you must have a general file, discard irrelevant items periodically, and make new filing categories and folders for documents that should be filed separately.

• Purge lengthy reports from your files as soon as possible to make room for new ones. Don't hoard old copies of updated reports or those that are obsolete.

These actions will keep your in-basket molehill from growing into a mountain.

BASIC TIME-SAVING TIPS

You need to do more than slay the paperwork dragon. Applying the valuable techniques that follow will help you keep track of items that need future attention, minimize interruptions, organize your work area, and account for how you use time.

• *Keep a bring-up file* to ensure that important items will surface on the date when action is needed. "A bring-up file is one of the most valuable time-management suggestions I ever heard," says one business professor and writer on management skills. "I picked up the idea from John, an old-timer I worked with in my first management job. He had a collapsible file folder with pockets numbered from 1 through 31 in his bottom desk drawer, and he filed items that needed follow-up according to their action date. He checked his folder every morning for items he needed to work on that day. I never saw him overlook or misplace a single item in two years."

• *Organize your desk and work area for maximum efficiency.* Place file cabinets, wastebasket, reference books, and other frequently used items within arm's length if possible. If you have a cubicle or office, position your desk out of sight of passersby to discourage idle conversation and drop-in visitors.

• *Keep a time log in a pocket notebook* to help you analyze how and where you spend your time and how it might be spent more efficiently. Jot down the nature of what you're doing every hour or two for several days so you can identify activities that eat up most of your time ("met with maintenance crew," "supervisors' meeting," "returned phone calls," "wrote/read correspondence," "set up overtime schedule," "rescheduled Owens job," "prepared budget," "ordered materials," etc.). Once you've identified your most time-consuming tasks, classify them (paperwork, meetings, scheduling, filling out forms, etc.). Then pinpoint (1) those that you can do more efficiently, (2) delegate to staff, or (3) cluster together and do all at once because they're complementary (for example, do both correspondence and telephone work at your desk as opposed to tasks that require you to get out on the floor and meet with others).

• *Use fragmented time productively.* Fragmented time is the five or ten minutes you might spend waiting for a meeting to start or a new work shift to take over. Do not disregard the value of these scattered chunks of time; minutes add up to hours, and hours add up to . . . well, you know the rest. If you use these scraps productively—to reflect on current problems, mentally review the status of rush jobs, edit a memo or report, rough out next week's work schedule—their total value can be impressive.

• *Manage your open-door policy.* An open door can be an invitation to chaos. You can't afford to be aloof or inaccessible, but you may need to manage your accessibility if you want to get any work done.

There's no simple open-door formula. Some managers set aside a specific time every day to meet with employees who need information or advice. Other managers have a hideout—a vacant office or cubicle to retreat to when they need to concentrate on an assignment without interruption. If neither of these ideas works for you, consider keeping your door partially closed (if you have an office) so people have to make a deliberate effort to interrupt you.

If you don't have an office, note important information that people tell you so you can follow up later, after you've finished the task at hand. Also delegate as much authority as possible (more on this in Chapter 7) so subordinates can make routine, simple decisions without your blessing. In addition, make it a habit to ask workers to propose solutions of their own for problems they bring you—not just dump them in your lap and run. Once word gets around, your staff should be more prone to think for themselves before interrupting you for advice.

• *Manage your telephone time.* If you usually have lots of calls to return, organize your day so you can return most or all of them at one sitting. If you need to stake out some quiet time, turn down the ringer or even unplug the telephone from the jack. If policy permits, consider using an answering machine to screen calls at your desk and decide which ones to take and which to return later.

You can also convert the telephone into an asset. Substitute a call for face-to-face discussions with individual workers whenever possible, and use conference calls instead of summoning everyone together for face-to-face meetings.

• *Master effective reading techniques.* The avalanche of in-house correspondence and management articles and books you'll encounter demands that you hone your reading efficiency to a razor's edge. How can you stay abreast of all the reading that piles up in your in-basket? Here's a four-stage process recommended by Phyllis Mindell, based on her book *Power Reading:*

1. Scan the material, looking for key words or phrases that relate to your job. If you find them or believe you need more information from the document, go back and skim it.

> **Yesterday is a canceled check; tomorrow is a promissory note; today is the only cash you have—so spend it wisely.**
>
> **—KAY LYONS**

2. Skimming (basically speed reading) gives you the gist of the contents. Note the piece's structural or skeletal elements such as the subject, title, subtitle, and subheadings. Skimming helps you decide which items are important enough to preread.

3. Preread the items that survived scanning and skimming by underlining key words and phrases in the text. Read precisely, paying special attention to the thesis statement or opening paragraph, the summary or conclusion, and each paragraph's topic sentence (which usually appears first). Few items—perhaps only one out of ten—deserve to advance to the fourth stage of deep reading.

4. Deep-read material by making notes in the margin, reflecting on the writer's message, searching for details, and decoding complex sentences. Read critically and skeptically; compare the writer's position with your own experience and opinions other people have expressed on the subject. Jot down your agreement or disagreement, comparisons, and other reactions in the margins. Dissect the material as objectively as possible.

REVIEW AND REFLECT

Put It in Focus

1. List your greatest actual or expected time wasters associated with your new job, along with ideas about how to deal with them.

_____

_____

_____

2. Prioritize and describe how you would handle the following situations:

   a. A key employee asks to take tomorrow off for a family emergency.

_____

_____

b. Your boss calls to announce a nonscheduled supervisors' meeting for 4 P.M. this afternoon.

_____

_____

c. You must review and approve your employees' regular monthly request for materials and supplies.

_____

_____

d. A worker drops in to warn you about the impending breakdown of a critical machine.

_____

_____

e. A teacher at a local high school called and left a message asking you to serve on the advisory board for one of its vocational programs.

_____

_____

f. Your boss asks you to submit a list tomorrow morning of your major accomplishments last quarter and your goals for this quarter.

_____

_____

g. A routine report is due in two weeks. It requires that you get information from each employee in your department.

_____

_____

h. Your boss calls and asks you to investigate a former subordinate's claim that she was sexually harassed by a coworker.

_____

_____

i. A colleague in another department asks you to gather information from your files that she needs to prepare a report for her supervisor.

_____

_____

j. Your boss asks you to review a copy of the proposed department budget for next fiscal year and recommend changes.

_____

_____

Matching

Match the action item in the left column with the recommended time management technique(s) in the right column. Place the letter(s) in the space next to the number it corresponds to.

Action Item	Technique
____ a. Weekly production report	1. Use fragmented time
____ b. Monthly overtime report	2. Chart or other aid
____ c. Monitor progress of a project due in six months	3. Delegation
____ d. Analyze how and where most time is spent	4. Conference call
____ e. Edit a memo or report	5. Bring-up file
____ f. Develop next week's work schedule	6. Find a hideout
____ g. Have workers make more routine decisions	7. Time log
____ h. Reserve some interrupted work time	8. "Boilerplate" correspondence
____ i. Gather information from several employees ASAP	

CHAPTER 3

SETTING GOALS AND PLANNING

Successful plans start with clear-cut goals; if you don't know where you're going, any road will take you there.

Goals answer the question, "What do I *really* want to do?" Express them in numbers for maximum objectivity. Numerical goals leave no debate about whether they were reached. If you can't quantify a goal precisely, set a minimum target that you plan to hit—for example, "Our department's goal is to reduce customer complaints by at least 10 percent next quarter"; "We intend to cut rework and scrap by at least 15 percent this month."

INVOLVING STAFF

Make your workers stakeholders in your department. If you involve them in setting goals, they'll be more likely to support those goals as a team instead of as a collection of individuals.

A retired executive who bought a doughnut shop had $5,000 to spend on improvements. "It would have been easy to walk in and tell my employees what I thought we should buy," he said, "but I thought, 'Why not let *them* decide?' After all, they had to work there all day. So I told them how much I could afford to spend and said, 'Spend it however you want. Just make sure that what you do makes life easier, faster, or better for yourselves or our customers.' "

His workers grabbed the ball and ran with it. They found some excellent bargains in secondhand mixing equipment, had conveyor shutoff switches installed at various places

When you give staff a vested interest in setting goals, they tend to work for themselves as well as for you. Enlightened self-interest can be a powerful motivator.

around the room (previously there was only one), and suggested several economical and logical ways to improve drive-in service and spruce up the building, inside and outside.

When you give staff a vested interest in setting goals, they tend to work for themselves as well as for you. Enlightened self-interest can be a powerful motivator.

PRACTICAL PRINCIPLES OF PLANNING

Goals are like destinations on a road map; plans are the routes you can take to reach them. Once you decide what you want to do, it's time to develop plans to get you from where you are to where you want to be.

Decide *what* must be done, by *whom*, *when*, and *how*. Then assign responsibility to your employees. You may have to inform them both verbally and in writing, depending on how complex the work is going to be.

Emphasize the tangible group and individual benefits your plans are meant to produce—for example, reduced fatigue or effort; greater productivity; increased earnings; savings in cost, time, or materials; increased job security; and the satisfaction of belonging to a winning team.

Give them every opportunity to ask questions; don't assume they understand instructions the first time you give them. As you've probably heard elsewhere, dumb questions are easier to handle than stupid mistakes. Once you've made the work assignments, give your workers enough authority to carry out their duties without interrupting you unnecessarily. Then hold follow-up meetings as necessary to clarify instruction, answer questions, and get feedback.

As work proceeds, generate a spirit of competition and commitment among the members of your group by pointing out the success and recognition other departments or competitors achieved from similar ventures. Knowing that others have blazed a trail assures staff that they're not being asked to do the impossible or pursue results on paper that haven't been tested elsewhere. If you're involved in a pilot project or programs such as total quality management or just-in-time inventory management that your organization is implementing for the first time, it's especially important to create a sense of esprit de corps and teamwork among employees (more on this in Chapter 5). People who have helped to set challenging goals and create the plans to carry them out tend to invest their best efforts to ensure success.

MINIMIZING CONTROLS

Controls measure the pulse of progress, but don't let the tail wag the dog. Too much red tape (reports, status meetings, and other bureaucratic flak) strangles employees' initiative and creativity. And if controls become an end in themselves instead of a means to an end, they are a burden on everyone.

The controls you decide on to monitor work—meetings, status reports, personal observation, quality assurance inspectors and equipment, guidelines expressed in policies and procedures, budgets, and employee performance evaluations—depend on the nature of the plans themselves and the work being done.

Give your group as much freedom as possible to use their own initiative, employ their own methods, apply their own ingenuity, and monitor and report on their progress with minimal attention and direction from you.

What makes a sound control device? The best controls ought to:

• *Identify and report problems without delay*. The space shuttle Challenger's computers were the first to sense a problem with the mission. They responded by swiveling the engine nozzles around as far as possible, attempting to make an in-flight correction, before the spacecraft exploded.

The difference between a minor glitch and a full-blown catastrophe often hinges on how much time goes by before somebody notices a problem. The best controls flag potential

> You've got to think about "big things" while you're doing small things so that all the small things go in the right direction.
>
> —ALVIN TOFFLER

trouble (e.g., numerical control devices that oversee and report the performance of automated production equipment).

• *Be objective.* A control device is worthless if people can manipulate it to make themselves look good. Objective controls report identical results no matter who is using them. Budgets, go/no-go gauges, and security systems that film shoplifters on videotape are examples of highly objective controls.

Employee performance ratings that are based on vague standards or on standards that managers may define however they wish suffer from a lack of objectivity. At a minimum, a sound evaluation system should describe the nature, extent, quality, and thoroughness of performance that deserves to be rated "excellent" as compared to "good," "fair," or "needs to improve."

Supervisors who ask employees to rate themselves as part of the performance evaluation process must realize that people aren't likely to evaluate their own performance objectively. It's like someone who tells a friend, "According to the scales my weight is fine, but the chart says I'm six inches too short."

• *Be easy to understand.* If controls are complicated or confusing, people will avoid using them whenever possible. Make sure that status reports, approval forms, and quality assurance equipment, for instance, are straightforward.

• *Be cost-effective.* A control device should cost less than potential losses from the condition it regulates. For example, many fast-food restaurants now let customers pour their own soft drinks. Management found that the cost of having employees fill and serve each drink was greater than the losses from customers who help themselves to free refills.

Managers in one company, distressed by employee pilferage, considered hiring more security guards but realized the salaries for the additional guards exceeded the cost of the inventory shrinkage. Instead, they simply told employees how the pilferage affected the company's profitability and therefore the value of the company's stock. Since most employees participated in the employee stock ownership plan, the pilferage rate dropped considerably after that.

REPORTING PROGRESS WITH VISUAL AIDS

Use line graphs, bar charts, time lines, and other graphics to track what's happening and to serve as a rallying point for workers' energy and commitment. In addition, visual aids will:

- Keep the team's collective efforts focused and unified.
- Give your group a sense of momentum and progress.
- Let everyone in your area confirm the status of major jobs whenever they wish (instead of having to attend a meeting, read a report, or interrupt you).

Update visual aids often and whenever a significant change occurs.

ARE YOU READY?

Use the following checklist for goals and plans:

☐ Have you set and communicated clear goals?

☐ Do those who will carry out your plans understand and support the goals behind them?

☐ Are your goals and plans compatible with those set by higher management and by other departments you work closely with?

☐ Are your plans flexible enough to permit changes if circumstances require them?

☐ Are your controls designed to monitor progress adequately without being too detailed or complicated?

REVIEW AND REFLECT

What's Next?

1. State briefly the three most important goals you would like your department to accomplish within the next ____ weeks.

   a. _____

   b. _____

   c. _____

2. Which employees should participate in clarifying and quantifying each of these goals? What specifically can you do to obtain their commitment and make them feel a personal stake in the outcome?

   Goal 1: _____

   _____

   _____

   Goal 2: _____

   _____

   _____

   Goal 3: _____

   _____

   _____

3. What specific responsibilities will you assign to each worker? How will you make their work assignments and encourage feedback and questions?

   Goal 1: _____

   _____

   _____

   Goal 2: _____

   _____

   _____

Goal 3: _____

_____

_____

4. What control devices will you use to monitor prog-
    ress toward each goal? Explain your choices.

    Goal 1: _____

    _____

    _____

    Goal 2: _____

    _____

    _____

    Goal 3: _____

    _____

    _____

How Do You Rate?

Rate yourself on each of the following characteristics.
Make a special note of those that you either lack or
need to improve. Be honest!

GOAL SETTING AND PLANNING

	Yes	No	Need to Improve
a. I'm comfortable sitting down with my staff to discuss group goals.	_____	_____	_____
b. I'm patient when people ask me questions about the instructions I give them.	_____	_____	_____
c. I give clear verbal instructions.	_____	_____	_____
d. I give clear written instructions.	_____	_____	_____

	Yes	No	Need to Improve
e. I enjoy selling people on the importance and benefits of making a new idea succeed.	_____	_____	_____
f. I have trouble letting others work on their own, without a lot of input and direction from me.	_____	_____	_____

What's Next?

Evaluate your answers to the How Do You Rate? checklist. Propose at least two specific actions you can take, starting tomorrow, to strengthen or eliminate each deficiency.

_____

_____

_____

_____

_____

_____

_____

_____

CHAPTER 4

LEADING YOUR PEOPLE

Effective leaders wear many hats. You'll be expected to serve as a role model for the people who work for you, coordinate their work, resolve their conflicts, promote their growth and development, represent them and your department to higher management and outside groups, and motivate them to achieve superior performance.

Good leaders aren't born. They develop and evolve through hard work, consistent effort, and an awareness of several factors that influence their success.

DETERMINE YOUR LEADERSHIP STYLE

Some authorities place leaders into one of three categories: autocratic, democratic, or laissez-faire. As this chapter unfolds, however, you will realize that there's no one best approach to leading your people.

How do these three leaders differ from each other?

Autocratic Leaders

Autocratic leaders tend to be highly opinionated and militaristic. Their consistent "I'm paid to think; you're paid to work" attitude, however, rarely gets the best performance from employees, because most workers don't like to be treated as androids or interchangeable parts. Moreover, autocratic leaders deny themselves the suggestions from and viewpoints of others that are often very helpful when figuring out how to solve a problem or tackle a new opportunity.

24

It wouldn't be right to say that you should never be an autocrat, though. For example, if you're training an inexperienced employee or dealing with unmotivated or indifferent workers, you may have to use an autocratic approach, at least temporarily. An autocratic leadership style may also be called for when workers must follow highly detailed, critical, or inflexible procedures such as those involved in assembling components that go into the space shuttle.

Democratic Leaders

Democratic leaders, by contrast, see themselves and their employees as a team. Their slogan might be, "We're paid to think and work as a unit." Most people would rather work for democratic than autocratic leaders, and democratic supervisors tend to get the full benefit of their staff members' ideas, opinions, and views. Supervisors who use this participative, team-oriented style tend to need more time to solve problems or analyze opportunities, however, because they negotiate, discuss, and consult with their teams as much as possible before making a decision.

Laissez-Faire Leaders

Laissez-faire leaders provide general direction and overall guidance, but they give their staff as much freedom as possible. A laissez-faire boss might say, "Do this however you want, as long as you get the results we need and don't violate company policy." This hands-off leadership style may work well with highly trained, self-motivated workers who neither need nor want close supervision.

Distance may force some managers to be laissez-faire leaders, too. For example, if you're supervising people who work at several different locations or travel a great deal, geography alone may dictate a free-rein approach because it would be physically impossible to stay on top of what each worker is doing all the time, every day. Employment decisions can be vitally important in these cases. When distance is a factor, you must hire self-directed, mature people who can be trusted to manage their time, work schedules, and duties responsibly with minimal guidance from you. Laissez-faire supervisors tend to have a great deal of confidence in their employees' abilities and judgment.

AVOID LEADERSHIP LAND MINES

Managers who have developed reputations as successful leaders didn't just luck into them. Part of their success can be credited to recognizing and avoiding several common pitfalls:

• *The belief that one leadership style fits every person and situation.* Managers who use only one approach to leading cannot get the best performance from everyone, because individuals react differently to different leadership styles and their reactions may be either positive or negative.

• *A tendency to be overly autocratic or dictatorial.* Although an autocratic approach demands the least amount of effort and conscious thought, employees are generally excluded from the decision-making process except as tools to carry out what the boss thinks should be done. Managers who take it upon themselves to define problems and decide how to solve them sometimes run themselves out on a limb and end up sawing it off.

• *A tendency to adopt the same approach to leadership one of your more impressive former managers used.* The trouble with this is that you're leading an entirely different group of people under a different set of circumstances than your role model faced.

It's important to let your own technique evolve and take shape and base it on the nature of your group and the types of problems and challenges that your job presents. You can't—and shouldn't—be a clone of a previous boss, no matter how exceptional he or she might have been.

CONSIDER THE INDIVIDUAL

One of the two most important factors to consider if you want to lead effectively is to get to know your people as individuals and apply the leadership style that is most likely to get the best performance from each one. Modifying your leadership style to accommodate individual differences takes some focused effort on your part, but the payoff in superior performance is worth it. Consider each person's previous experience, training, initiative, ambition, and apparent motivation. For example, you might give employees who possess a generous amount of those qualities minimal direction and control and relatively brief instructions when making an assignment. A more autocratic approach might be called for if you're working with relatively new workers, those who lack self-confidence, or people whose past performance shows that they need detailed instructions and close supervision.

One management consultant recalls, "The most difficult question I was ever asked in a seminar was, 'How do I get my boss to lead me the way I want to be led?' This came from an employee who deserved and needed to be led democratically but worked for a habitual autocrat who wouldn't change his style for anything or anyone. The worker who talked with me was the best producer in the group, but her supervisor's leadership approach was killing her spirit. Every morning was a line-up-for-inspection and "Here is how you'll do it" affair. This treatment was so incompatible with her personality and abilities that she was on the verge of resigning. The company was about to lose one of its best employees because of an inflexible leader.

"I frankly didn't know how to answer her question," the consultant says, "but it certainly made me remember to tell every supervisor this: *Be willing to change your approach to match to your people.*"

CONSIDER THE SITUATION

The second most important factor that developing leaders should consider is that some situations, like some people, deserve to be led differently. For example, crises or nonnegotiable deadlines may require an autocratic approach.

Someone has to step in, take charge, make decisions, allocate resources, assign responsibilities, and ensure that the work gets done right and on time. If you're dealing with noncritical situations or routine tasks that are clearly covered by policies and procedures, you can afford to scale back to a more democratic or perhaps a laissez-faire approach.

EMPHASIZE RESULTS OVER METHODS

Some leaders are too prescriptive. They become obsessed with the techniques or approaches employees use to do the work instead of focusing on the results they're supposed to achieve.

The next time you make an assignment, try this: Tell your people *what* you expect, but leave most or all of the decisions about *how* they should do it up to them. This takes some courage, but the results might surprise you. When supervisors give workers the latitude to let their creativity flow, marvelous things can happen. When it comes right down to it, why should you care which methods your team uses as long as the work gets done correctly, on time, within budget, and without violating company policy?

Supervisors who emphasize results over methods . . . empower workers to think to the best of their abilities and employ their own resources all day, every day, for the benefit of everyone.

Supervisors who emphasize results over methods develop confident, competent subordinates who think for themselves and approach problems creatively. They empower workers to think to the best of their abilities and employ their own resources all day, every day, for the benefit of everyone.

KEEP IN TOUCH WITH YOUR TROOPS

People respect leaders who communicate directly with them. You've got to see and be seen; manage by walking around. Managers who appear to be aloof or too busy or who isolate themselves behind desks, walls, or secretaries sometimes earn contempt from the rank and file.

When you keep in touch with your troops, you can sense

the rhythm and flow of the workplace and what's going on. This practice is sometimes infinitely more valuable than relying on written reports and occasional comments from people who happen to drop by. An added benefit is that your employees will respect you for making the effort to get out and circulate among them and to listen to their comments, both positive and negative.

A textile company executive, recalling his days as a management trainee, had a supervisor who started out in one of the lowest-paid jobs in the company and rose up through the ranks to become a plant manager.

"I noticed during my first week that Mike walked through every department in the plant at least once a day. He called it his plant tour. One day I asked him why he did it, especially when he had so many problems to sort out back in his office. He said it was the most important thing he did.

" 'I want them to know I care—*really* care—about what's going on out there,' he said. 'When they see me face to face, it reinforces my sincerity and concern about all of us doing a good job. Oh, my supervisors keep me posted about lots of what goes on, but it's just not the same as seeing it firsthand. There's also the possibility that they might gloss over problems or try to keep a lid on them, hoping that they'll be able to put out the fire before I smell the smoke. But I don't want that, and I don't want our employees to think I'm too busy to stay in touch with what's really going on.' "

The same philosophy is as true in sports as in business. Barely two decades ago a well-known southern university with a struggling football program hired a head coach who coached from the press box instead of the sidelines. Although this gave him a better perspective during the game, the team, fans, and alumni became contemptuous and disgusted about his remote-control technique. His first two years produced four wins, eighteen losses, and serious talk of dissolving the entire football program. In desperation, the university recruited a new coach, one known for his rapport and involvement with players, a reputation earned in part because he coached from the sidelines and stayed close to his team. At last count, coach Bobby Bowden's record at Florida State University was 165–46–3, including a 1993 national championship, two consecutive Atlantic Coast Conference championships, and seven consecutive top-four finishes in the AP Poll. The mountain of awards his players have won includes two Butkus awards and one Heisman trophy.

DEVELOPING YOUR ROLE AS COACH AND COUNSELOR

Effective leaders are inherently effective coaches. What makes them so are several key qualities:

- They keep their workers' energy and efforts focused on clear goals that everyone understands and supports.
- They generate and promote enthusiasm, self-confidence, and pride.
- They teach employees that frustration and failure can fuel a drive toward superior performance and success when the next set of opportunities arises.
- They lead people to believe in and embrace the benefits that come from self-discipline, hard work, dedication to purpose, and a unified sense of purpose.
- They challenge and help employees to cultivate their individual skills to a razor's edge while channeling those skills toward goals that promote the success and reputation of the group as well as its members.

REVIEW AND REFLECT

How Do You Rate?

Rate yourself on each of the following qualities. Make a special note of those that you either lack or need to improve. Be honest!

> The techniques of leadership are admittedly the most mysterious and the most difficult to teach. Yet, in the long run, the very fact that (you are) trying to be a good leader shows through. People become what they seek to be.
>
> —FREDERICK C. AND JOHN M. DYER IN *The Enjoyment of Management*

LEADERSHIP QUALITIES

	Yes	No	Need to Improve
a. I'm comfortable giving direct orders and acting assertively when necessary.	___	___	___
b. I can work as a collaborator, coach, and colleague with my group when the situation requires it.	___	___	___
c. I have little difficulty allowing others to use their own judgment and employ their own methods to do a job.	___	___	___
d. I prefer to supervise people directly rather than from a distance.	___	___	___
e. I would rather let workers decide how to do a job than dictate to them how to go about it.	___	___	___

True/False and Multiple Choice

Answer the true/false statements by placing a "T" or "F" in the space provided. Answer the multiple-choice questions by circling the number of the best answer.

a. Which of the following statements is true of leadership styles?
   1. No style is ideal.
   2. Managers should be autocratic leaders as much as possible, because employees expect and respond to close supervision.
   3. A democratic leadership style is generally the best to use when dealing with a crisis.
   4. Experienced, mature subordinates react negatively to laissez-faire leaders.

b. ___ The most effective leaders use one style of leadership consistently.

c. ___ Successful leaders get to know their employees as individuals.

d. Which of the following situations would generally require an autocratic leadership style?
   1. "This project has a three-week deadline; it's identical to the one you completed in ten days last month."
   2. "I'm going to assign Mary to that job; she has done it several times in the past three months."
   3. "I've just hired a bright, ambitious new assistant, but he has no experience with the type of work we do here."
   4. "I'm not quite sure how to set up the schedule for this production run, but several of my people have done that type of thing before."

e. Which of the following situations would generally require a democratic leadership style?
   1. "If we don't ship this order by 3:00 P.M. tomorrow, we'll lose the contract and have to lay off 15 percent of our workforce."
   2. "Higher management has changed the frequency of your activity report from every two weeks to once a month, but the format is the same as before."
   3. "I'm not certain what's causing the problem; it could be traced to several areas in my department."
   4. "Mike says he understands our rules on lateness, but he has clocked in ten to fifteen minutes late on four of the last eight workdays."

f. Which of the following situations would generally require a laissez-faire leadership style?
   1. "Jack isn't a total expert on this type of work. I'm putting him on the job because the experience will help him increase his knowledge and promotability."

2. "I've found that Janet lacks the self-confidence to tackle an assignment like that without occasional guidance from me."

3. "Data processing says the new minicomputer must be installed where Bob's desk is in order to hook up the cabling correctly."

4. "You can go to lunch whenever you've restocked the shelves and set up the equipment for the orders we're going to run this afternoon."

What's Next?

Evaluate each of your employees in the light of the leadership information you've learned in this chapter. First consider such factors as training, ambition, self-motivation, experience, listening skills, self-confidence, initiative, and temperament. Then select a leadership style that would *generally* seem to be most effective for each person. Briefly justify your answer.

Name: _____

    Most effective style: _____

_____

Name: _____

    Most effective style: _____

_____

Name: _____

    Most effective style: _____

_____

Name: _____

    Most effective style: _____

_____

Name: _____

    Most effective style: _____

_____

CHAPTER 5

TEAM BUILDING

Teamwork. It's more than a fad or a buzzword. Interactive work teams have become a way of doing business, and supervisors who want to succeed in today's management climate must learn to build and use work teams as a way of life.

WHY USE TEAMS?

Work teams increase unity and a sense of purpose among employees. Teamwork gives them a greater sense of identity and a collective, contagious pride in their performance. People feel gratified and rewarded when they're members of a winning team. In addition, you'll spend less time directing traffic, making assignments, and arbitrating disagreements among employees who work as semiautonomous units.

HOW CAN YOU USE TEAMS?

There are several practical ways to apply teamwork in a group or department:

• *Decision making*. As a manager, you can use teams to assist you with decision making in several ways. They can (1) gather, analyze, and summarize information about problems or opportunities; (2) recommend several potential solutions based on information they have assembled; or, the ultimate step, (3) actually decide certain issues as a group and implement the decision. Decision-making teams with these various degrees of authority could be used, for example, to resolve production bottlenecks, improve customer service, streamline paperwork flow or work layout, or reduce machine downtime for preventive maintenance or model changeovers.

• *Production.* Production teams have long been used by such companies as Saab and Volvo. Team members are cross-trained to do a variety of tasks, which maximizes flexibility, minimizes boredom, and may increase employees' job security. Cross-training may not be practical if members' tasks are highly specialized (such as the work of space shuttle teams and race car pit crews).

• *Project or product development.* Team members from a variety of departments—usually marketing, design, engineering, manufacturing, purchasing, and finance—join forces to develop and test prototypes or bring a new model to market. Managers at Ford Motor Company created such cross-functional teams to develop new models of the Probe, Thunderbird, and Mustang. Team members worked together at the same location and reported to one project manager instead of to the managers of their individual functions.

• *Changeover or transition teams.* Teams may be assembled to coordinate the efforts of various departments that must work together to install new systems, procedures, or equipment. In such cases the team serves as a steering committee to oversee the direction and implementation of the change.

WHAT ARE THE BASIC GUIDELINES?

Work teams succeed and flourish when managers and team members work hard and pull together. Here are some guidelines to help you build and work with teams:

• *Set goals as a team.* This collective approach helps to ensure that everyone accepts and supports the group's decisions. People feel they have a stake in and a personal commitment to goals they've had a hand in setting. Make sure the team defines its goals clearly and quantifies these goals whenever possible. The more precise the goal is, the better that team members can monitor and assess progress as they focus their energy and resources on reaching it.

• *Reward group performance over individual performance.* Group rewards encourage team members to police each other's work; bond members' loyalty to the team and motivate each member not to be the weak link in the chain; and motivate team members to be mutually supportive, rally behind each other's efforts, and unite to eliminate problems that may jeopardize the group's success.

Your group reward system must include frequent feedback on the team's performance, so members can monitor their collective progress and take fast action when things go haywire. An eye-catching chart, graph, or other visual aid often fills the bill.

Group rewards are limited only by ingenuity and budget. They may include public praise, a bonus to be shared among team members, a rotating trophy that is temporarily "owned" by the best-performing team, or assignment to a more desirable work shift or project.

• *Cross-train team members whenever feasible.* Cross-training permits members to trade off responsibilities, and that alleviates boredom and monotony. You may find that workers become so proficient that you can let them distribute certain tasks among themselves or decide which jobs each one will do during a shift.

• *Become a sounding board, constructive critic, and adviser.* Some managers have difficulty accepting the idea that they're no longer "the boss" in the traditional sense, but it's absolutely vital to the success of the team. Organizations that apply teamwork successfully have transformed managers into facilitators who ensure that each work team has all the information and resources it needs to do its job. The supervisor no longer controls the group, because everyone becomes responsible for results. In teamwork, a manager is a guide on the side, not a sage on the stage. In some companies, teams elect their own leaders from among the ranks and rotate the job of leader periodically.

In team-work, a manager is a guide on the side, not a sage on the stage.

- *Don't let teams become isolated from each other.* Make sure that they coordinate and synchronize their efforts with other key parties and groups inside and outside your department that may depend on them for input, output, or information. In this way, a sense of unity will infect not only the members of a single team but spread among all teams. Their collective and mutually supportive efforts benefit the entire organization.

- *Keep teams relatively small.* Small teams pose fewer coordination and communication problems, reach agreement and consensus more easily, and tend to bond more closely than members of large groups (which often form factions and splinter groups within themselves).

- *Promote a team identity.* Badges, caps, jackets, patches, decals, or other insignia encourage cohensiveness and a feeling of combined purpose.

- *Select members who have both complementary and counterbalancing views and skills.* This may mean, for example, deliberately combining positive thinkers and skeptics, freethinking innovators and regimented pragmatists, dreamers and doers. Such a mix gives the team an internal system of checks and balances on its members' actions and decisions.

- *Provide training.* Throw a bunch of individuals together haphazardly, and you may get nothing but collective chaos. Be alert to a team's need for training in such areas as:

    —Decision making
    —Avoiding groupthink (the tendency for some members to defer to the majority or certain opinion leaders instead of challenging their assumptions or position)
    —Acknowledging and respecting opposing viewpoints (disagreeing without being disagreeable)
    —Accepting differences in each other's ethnic background, work experience, personalities, and other factors that may distract some members from the team's collective mission

- *Be patient.* It takes time—two years or even longer— for a work team to galvanize into a unified, productive, self-directed unit. The transition to work teams represents a fundamental shift in organizational tradition, philosophy, and culture. Success won't happen overnight.

TEAMWORK ISN'T FOR EVERYONE

One step by 100 persons is better than 100 steps by one person.

—KOICHI TSUKAMOTO

Not all employees are temperamentally suited for team membership and group efforts, despite whatever training or other measures you've applied. You may need to transfer these lone wolves to more traditional departments or tasks where their tendencies won't impede (and may actually enhance) their success.

Occasionally an employee may be openly hostile to the idea of working as a member of a team or sharing group rewards. If that's the case and if you've exhausted all efforts to find a suitable position that accommodates the person's skills and abilities, you may have little choice except discharge.

REVIEW AND REFLECT

True/False and Multiple Choice

Answer the true/false statements by placing a "T" or "F" in the space provided. Answer the multiple-choice questions by circling the number of the best answer.

a. _____ Work teams are generally inappropriate for gathering problem-solving information.

b. _____ It's often feasible to cross-train team members to do several jobs.

c. _____ Teams may be responsible for both planning and executing a new product's development.

d. _____ Team goals should not be quantified unless absolutely necessary.

e. _____ When developing work teams, managers should reward individual performance over group performance.

f. _____ Teams tend to succeed best when they receive frequent feedback on performance.

g. _____ Managers of work teams often do more facilitating and guiding than supervising and controlling.

h. _____ It's relatively unimportant for work teams to coordinate their efforts with teams outside their department.

i. _____ The smaller the team is, the greater are the odds for success.

j. _____ Teams tend to work best when their members share similar skills and viewpoints.

k. _____ Management should expect to realize the benefits of work teams within several weeks of their formation.

l. Which of the following is *least* true about work teams?
   1. They increase cohesiveness among members.
   2. They give employees a greater sense of identity and autonomy.
   3. They promote a collective pride of performance.
   4. They require managers to spend more time making assignments.

m. When developing and using work teams:
   1. Define goals in general rather than specific terms.
   2. Let proficient teams allocate the tasks among themselves.
   3. Provide cross-training for teams that do highly specialized or critical work.
   4. Never put innovators and pragmatists on the same team.

n. Managers who want to use teamwork:
   1. Must be active, involved leaders who oversee and control each team member's work.
   2. Must be scavengers who provide whatever infor-

mation and resources team members need to do their jobs.

3. Should not empower a team to both decide and implement a decision.

4. Should set team goals themselves, but allow team members to decide how to reach those goals.

Brainstormer's Corner

Summarize your department's major roles, goals, and responsibilities. Then do the following exercises:

a. List three specific tasks in your area that seem to lend themselves to teamwork.

1. _____

2. _____

3. _____

b. What specific actions might you take, *starting to-morrow,* to begin assembling work teams to tackle those three tasks?

Task 1: _____

Task 2: _____

Task 3: _____

c. What higher-management support should you obtain in order to proceed, from whom, and how might you get it?

Task 1: _____

_____

Task 2: _____

_____

Task 3: _____

_____

d. Do you think it's practical to ask for volunteers to begin each venture? Explain your answer for each task.

Task 1: _____

_____

Task 2: _____

_____

Task 3: _____

_____

e. Which specific employees seem most receptive to the idea of teamwork?

_____

_____

f. Which employees are likely to have a negative reaction to the idea of teamwork? For each one, jot down ways to counter his or her initial reaction.

Name: _____

Approach to use: _____

_____

Name: _____

Approach to use: _____

_____

Name: _____

Approach to use: _____

_____

Name: _____

Approach to use: _____

_____

Name: _____

Approach to use: _____

_____

Name: _____

Approach to use: _____

_____

CHAPTER 6

MAKING EFFECTIVE DECISIONS

Decisions are the landmarks of every manager's career.

Decisions are the landmarks of every manager's career. What you do about the problems and opportunities you meet in your job has a cumulative and often a comprehensive impact on your reputation and success.

Although this chapter focuses mainly on problem-oriented decisions, remember that the eight-step process set out here can also be applied, with few changes and equal success, when you're deciding any important matter.

THE DECISION-MAKING PROCESS

Step 1: Define the Problem

The success of every later step in the process depends on clearly answering this question: "What's *really* wrong?" If you're thoroughly familiar with the area where the problem is, ask the people who work there what they think is wrong. This is virtually always a good move, because when you involve those who will be troubleshooting a problem, you also give them a vested interest in solving it. So be a democratic leader; practice participative management. This approach can help you avoid false starts, backtracking, wheel spinning, and serious losses later on. Remember the ill-fated IBM PCjr? Its keyboard had a touch and key shape that felt odd to many users. Some believe this fiasco wouldn't have happened if management had let secretaries and other word processing employees use prototype models and asked for their opinions.

When you're trying to define a problem, don't be fooled by symptoms. Symptoms give you clues about what's wrong, but they're not solutions. For example, if rejects skyrocket in one department, that's a symptom, *not* the problem. The problem is what's *causing* those rejects—faulty materials, employee sabotage, improperly adjusted equipment, or a host of other possibilities. As another example, a flat tire on your car is merely a symptom. Pumping up the tire is a quick fix but not a genuine solution, because the tire will only go flat again. What caused the air to leak out is the real problem, and you (or a service station attendant) need to identify and fix it before your troubles will be over.

Step 2: Develop Alternative Solutions

Once you believe you've identified the true problem, generate as many solutions as possible. This step usually presents another good opportunity to involve your group by saying, "Now that we think we know what's wrong, what do we think we can do to fix it?"

If the nature of the problem and the time you have to solve it permit, a brainstorming session might be valuable here. Call together everyone who has a stake in solving the problem, and ask them to suggest any solution that comes to mind, no matter how bizarre or impractical it may seem. The ground rules of brainstorming demand a totally freewheeling meeting where nobody criticizes anyone else's comments and everyone feels free to suggest original solutions and build on or modify those proposed by other members of the group.

The goal of a brainstorming session is to generate as many potential solutions as possible, no matter how unusual they might be. It's usually easier to modify a wild idea into a workable solution than to try to pump life into a lukewarm suggestion that may produce mediocre results at best.

Ingenuity is the key. If you organize a brainstorming session, prohibit group members from voicing creativity killers:

"Don't be ridiculous."

"It's too early [late] for that."

"We've never tried that before."

"The union will complain."

"It's worked just fine until now."

"We can't afford it."

"Higher management would never okay it."

"It won't work in our department."

"That's not our problem."

Some managers set a ground rule that anyone who makes a negative or critical comment during a brainstorming session must pay a dollar into the kitty, with the money used to buy refreshments after the meeting.

Step 3: Evaluate Potential Solutions

The fun starts to fade away at this reality check. Here you screen the solutions you've produced against such limits as your budget; available people, time, and equipment; policies, procedures, and rules; and other factors beyond your control. This process of elimination weeds out actions that clearly can't be done, leaving several potential solutions on the table to carry forward.

Step 4: Let Things Incubate

Put your feet up on the desk and let the whole matter simmer on your mental back burner. If you've ever written a letter, put it away for a day or two, and reread it before you mailed it, you can appreciate the value of this step.

During this process of incubation, your mind consciously and subconsciously sorts things out and views the problem and possible solutions from different angles. Don't be surprised if a new solution or two comes to mind.

Good things may happen on your way to a decision if you let things simmer. If nothing else, incubation prevents you from making a snap decision, which is frequently the same as tossing a coin.

Step 5: Pick a Tentative Solution

You can't incubate a decision forever. Sooner or later, you have to decide which one of several potential solutions seems to be the best. Your choice will be based on information that you and your employees uncovered during Step 3 (evaluation) as well as the insights, perspectives, and modifications that may have surfaced since then.

Notice that this step mentions a *tentative* solution. That correctly implies that you should pilot-run the favored solution to a critical decision before you make a final commitment.

Step 6: Make a Pilot Run

Which decisions should you pilot-run? Generally any decision that could have a significant and negative impact on your career and reputation, the success of your employer and your department, and the careers and general welfare of your employees.

A pilot run or pretest uncovers bugs in a major decision and helps you fine-tune it before you go public with it. The logic is simple: You're safer to risk a little by testing a decision on a limited basis than to bet the rent while flying blind.

Savvy managers pilot-run high-risk decisions whenever possible. For example:

- Fast-food chains pilot-run new menu items extensively before going nationwide.
- Companies test new information-reporting and computer systems extensively before changing over from the old method.
- A new piece of production equipment may be installed and run parallel to the machine it will replace until all the kinks have been worked out.
- New employees may have to work through a probationary period before their employment becomes final.

Granted, some of these situations involve top management decisions and millions of dollars of potential profit or loss, but benefits of a pilot run are identical at lower levels.

A department manager in a large textile plant believed that new lighting would improve workers' visibility and thus raise the quality of their products, but the cost of new fixtures made the decision too risky without a pilot run. She installed new lights in 20 percent of the area, monitored product quality from those machines, and used the superior quality statistics to justify making the capital outlay.

Management of one manufacturing company once decided, without doing a pilot run, to attach meters to secretaries' typewriters and pay them according to the number of keys they struck during the day. The program was discontinued after secretaries were seen eating lunch with one hand and randomly banging away on their keyboards with the other.

The pilot run results may reveal that a decision should be modified in several ways. You may even discover that the decision that looked so good on paper bombed in practice and should be abandoned altogether. Regardless of the situation, a pilot run clarifies and minimizes the risks connected with making a key decision.

Step 7: Gain Support

Support from others is vital because you're rarely the only person involved in putting your decisions to work. Some otherwise sound decisions may be doomed to fail if the people who have to make them succeed refuse to support them beyond the letter of their job descriptions. But if your workers helped you define the problem and generated and evaluated possible solutions, you will enjoy a firm base of support.

Circumstances may suggest that you get your boss's endorsement too. This is especially true when your decision cuts across departmental boundaries or otherwise affects areas or employees who aren't under your control. Let's say one of your decisions requires several other departments to change the format or frequency of the periodic reports that they issue. Your peer managers in those departments might complain about the changes you want them to make in their routine, especially if more work is involved. But if you've convinced your boss that *your* decision is justified, they may have no choice in the matter.

Step 8: Follow Up and Confirm Results

A successful pilot run can raise your level of confidence but doesn't guarantee a successful overall result. After all, the experiment may have been poorly designed, conducted at the wrong time, or done in the wrong place. Don't assume too much from the pilot run.

Follow up to confirm that the solution is working out as well as the pilot run implied by asking those who are doing the hands-on implementation how things are going:

> "Are things generally working out the way we thought they would?"
>
> "What has caused new or unexpected problems with what we're doing? . . . What suggestions do you have for dealing with them?"
>
> "In what ways has our decision worked out better than we thought? . . . Why is this so?"
>
> "What changes should we make at this point to improve the results?"
>
> "If we try this approach again, what should we do differently? . . . What should we leave alone?"
>
> "Do you see other areas in our department or other departments where what we're doing would improve operations somehow?"

LIMITS ON AUTHORITY

Subordinates who are afraid to act on their own to carry out your decisions may try to bounce the ball back onto your court. Don't let that happen. Clarify how far each employee

Nothing creates more self-respect among employees than being included in the process of making decisions.

—JUDITH M. BARDWICK

can go without getting your approval. Remind workers who come back to your desk like homing pigeons to "touch base" or "get your input" that you neither want nor expect to be involved in the nuts and bolts of making the decision work. You may have involved them in deciding what to do, but now that that's done, give them the authority to decide how to do it. This approach develops more confident, competent, and promotable employees and frees you to learn and grow within the limits of your own job.

REVIEW AND REFLECT

True/False and Multiple Choice

Answer the true/false statements by placing a "T" or "F" in the space provided. Answer the multiple-choice questions by circling the number of the best answer.

a. ____ Sound decision making begins with developing alternative solutions.

b. ____ Competent managers should be able to define and solve problems without input from the people who work for them.

c. ____ Once a solution is pilot-run, it's too late to select an alternative.

d. ____ The decision-making process is complete after a manager gains support for the decision.

e. ____ Experienced managers should be able to implement decisions regardless of how subordinates react to them.

f. Which of the following questions must be answered during the first step in the decision-making process?
   1. "Who is going to implement it?"
   2. "What does higher management think?"
   3. "How much money can we afford to spend?"
   4. "What's *really* wrong?"

g. When you define a problem:
    1. Its cause will disappear if you eliminate the symptoms.
    2. Use an autocratic leadership style.
    3. The success of later steps in the process depends on what you do at this step.
    4. None of the above.

h. The technique of brainstorming:
    1. Requires group members to criticize each other's suggestions.
    2. Is best applied when following up on the success of a decision.
    3. Is practical only for higher-level management decisions.
    4. Should encourage members to propose as many ideas as possible.

i. If a proposed solution conflicts with organizational policy, the most practical course is to:
    1. Select an alternate solution.
    2. Have the policy changed.
    3. Ignore the conflict and proceed with implementing the decision.
    4. Postpone the decision.

j. The incubation step in decision making:
    1. Should be used only when time is very short.
    2. Ensures that the final decision will be an ideal one.
    3. Provides clarification and direction.
    4. Requires that you ask peers, your boss, and your employees for suggestions.

Put It to Work

Recall at least two memorable work-related decisions that were sound and two that weren't so sound. Compare the means by which you reached each one with the steps discussed in this chapter.

a.
    two sound decisions even more successful? Why?

_____

_____

_____

b. What have you learned that could have helped you
    decide differently in the situations that turned out
    poorly? Why?

    _____

    _____

    _____

Brainstormer's Corner

a. List at least three specific actions you can take,
    starting tomorrow, to involve your employees more
    fully in defining and clarifying problems and oppor-
    tunities in your department and recommending so-
    lutions and responses.

    _____

    _____

    _____

b. Which of these actions could be integrated with
    the teamwork concepts that you learned about in
    Chapter 5? How would you begin to do so?

    Action: _____
    Implementation: _____

    _____

    Action: _____
    Implementation: _____

    _____

    Action: _____
    Implementation: _____

    _____

CHAPTER 7

DELEGATING AUTHORITY

Delegation—passing down some of your authority to people who work for you—is one of the most valuable and versatile tools of the management trade. Unfortunately, many managers avoid it, fear it, or use it incorrectly because they:

- Worry that employees will make mistakes.
- Dislike sharing credit for success with subordinates.
- Believe they don't have time to teach workers how to do the delegated work.
- Don't trust the methods or techniques employees would use.
- Prefer to retain total control over their job by doing everything themselves.

You've probably had bosses in your career who didn't delegate, or did so reluctantly, for similar reasons. The trouble is, poor delegators are frequently ineffective managers because they deny themselves the major benefits of delegation:

- Having more time to solve unique problems and work on nonroutine tasks.
- Placing decision-making authority in the hands of those who are closest to the problems or opportunities in question.
- Developing confident, competent employees who think for themselves and require minimal supervision.
- Improving the manager's own chance for advancement by preparing one or more subordinates to take over the job when a promotion becomes available.

CHOOSING THE BEST PERSON FOR THE TASK

Delegation is more than just picking a warm body. Following an orderly, thoughtful selection routine helps you choose subordinates whose skills are most compatible with the job or pick those who should benefit most from the experience.

Analyze the Task and Candidates

Many supervisors underestimate the importance of doing this, but it's central to delegating work effectively. Consider the following factors:

• *How close is the deadline?* Rush jobs require time-oriented workers who can be counted on to come through under pressure. Consider candidates in the light of their self-management ability and sense of responsibility to themselves, to you, and to the organization. The tighter the deadline is, the more you'll need to choose a conscientious worker who will do the right thing and do it on time.

• *How much coordination is needed?* Delegate assignments that demand lots of coordination or cooperation among colleagues or departments to consensus builders. Jobs that call for little interaction with other departments, however, might safely be delegated to more headstrong, less diplomatic subordinates.

• *How will the job help the person to grow?* This is an excellent chance to help satisfy employees' training and development needs that come to light through performance evaluations. Check your files to identify subordinates who would benefit most from this assignment. Consider, for example, the degree of challenge posed by the task; how much initiative, judgment, or discretion it calls for; and how well it will help the candidate develop verbal or written communication skills.

• *How much innovation is involved?* Highly innovative assignments call for dreamers more than doers—people who, like the bird who built a nest with a hole in the bottom, thrive on creativity but dislike responsibility. On the other hand, tasks that involve a routine or plain old "grunt work" are best given to detail-minded systems builders who enjoy doing work that has been laid out for them.

Additionally, take time to weigh such factors as enthusiasm, ambition, and desire. Employees who get excited about learning new skills and mastering new techniques may do a better job than their more apathetic coworkers.

What If Several People Are Qualified?

This is a welcome dilemma, but one that must be handled fairly in order to preserve high morale. One solution is to let the employees themselves decide who will get the job. This tactic, while admittedly frustrating, gives them experience with consensus building, compromise, and group dynamics. Be sure to clarify that you've left the decision to them for those reasons, and *not* because you're reluctant to make it yourself or exercise leadership.

An obvious alternative is to pick the person yourself. If you do, make sure to promise those who were passed over that they'll get the next assignment that comes up.

Finally, you might let several equally qualified subordinates tackle the project as a team instead of assigning it to one person alone.

If there's no clear standout choice after you've analyzed the task and candidates, consider giving the job to the person (or perhaps a team of coworkers) who seems to need the experience most and/or possesses most of the skills that the job demands. Relative motivation may be an arbitrating factor here too.

Explain Your Decision

Once you've made your decision, explain its rationale to the runners-up. This action is important, because it minimizes claims of favoritism or discrimination. Be sure that everyone understands the criteria you used to make your selection and the reasons why you chose whom you did.

Each of us grows by being asked to stretch beyond our limits; you compliment your people when you expect more from them than they may think they're capable of.

DISCUSSING THE ASSIGNMENT

When you call in the person to discuss the assignment, highlight aspects of the project that may be especially challenging, but express your faith in the employee's ability to meet these challenges and grow with the experience. Each of us grows by being asked to stretch beyond our limits; you compliment your people when you expect more from them than they may think they're capable of.

Don't give the impression that the job is a sink-or-swim proposition. Be prepared to coach and be accessible, while taking care not to let the employee shift decisions onto your shoulders or use your availability as a crutch.

WHAT SHOULD YOU DO IF IT DOESN'T WORK?

Delegation is an inexact science. If you see the employee falling short of standards, making mistakes, or acting frustrated with the delegated task, don't act precipitously. Some thought on your part, plus help for the employee, may redeem the situation.

Review How You Made the Assignment

When you notice continuing signs of trouble, take a few minutes to review how you delegated the job in the first place. Did you:

- Set clear performance standards?
- Explain the how-to's of the job thoroughly?
- Actively solicit the worker's questions?
- Give the worker a model or example to measure performance against?
- Follow up after the task was assigned?

This exercise will help you troubleshoot your delegation technique (and perhaps correct some flaws), but you'll have to go further to resolve your immediate problem.

Resist the Urge to Recall the Entire Task

Your first urge might be to recall the job entirely and either do it yourself or assign it to someone else. Don't. Overreacting by taking back a task immediately can devastate a worker's ego and cause smoldering resentment because you deny him or her a chance to fix the problem and set things right. No one likes to lose face and be branded a failure in front of coworkers. Savvy supervisors, like seasoned football coaches, don't bench rookie players because of one miscue.

Beyond your employee's feelings, however, consider what you'd be doing to yourself. Rescinding authority at the first sign of trouble makes you look impulsive and indecisive. In addition, your approach to the problem sets a precedent as far as other workers are concerned. They'll see your response as a model for how they might be treated under the same circumstances, and they'll react in one of two ways. They may either (1) sidestep your efforts to delegate work (they won't want to be treated as incompetents if they, too, have trouble doing a new job correctly) or (2) be prone to do a careless job, knowing that you'll shift the burden back onto your own shoulders. As one employee put it, "Why should I worry about screwing up? The first time something goes wrong, my boss will jump in with both feet and do it himself!"

Work With the Confused Employee

Several steps can keep you from shooting from the hip or shooting yourself in the foot when delegation bogs down:

1. *Talk before you act.* Talk to the worker privately, reviewing performance standards and explaining why the work hasn't been acceptable. Be specific; avoid vague remarks like, "Things aren't working out" or "I think I'd better reconsider what I gave you to do last week." People are typically hungry for details when their pride and performance are on the line. They won't be satisfied with generalities. Would you?

This conference also gives you an opportunity to establish a sense of obligation and joint commitment. After all, both of you have a stake in the outcome and a shared interest in seeing that the job in question is done correctly.

Ask the employee to propose actions that might resolve the problem and tactfully suggest that more training, preparation, or authority might be in order. If the person feels ill equipped to do the task because of one of those factors, you've made it easier to say so. Without some encouragement, people are embarrassed to admit that they're treading water.

This is also an ideal time to review the how-to's of the job once again. Recap your original instructions carefully (avoid remarks like "This is self-explanatory") and welcome the employee's questions by asking open-ended questions of your own that presume you haven't explained everything clearly—for example:

"What else should we go over?"
"Which part of the job do we need to talk about some more?"
"What activities do you feel unclear about?"

If the delegated job has a tangible result that can be demonstrated (such as a properly formatted report or a specific production routine), set up an example that the employee can use as a model. This may be all that's necessary to eliminate confusion and put things back on an even keel.

If the job consists of a central task and several satellite tasks, your worker's comments during this meeting might suggest that you take back some of the lesser ones temporarily, giving the person more time to master the core task without getting lost in details. When saddled with a major responsibility and a host of secondary tasks, some people panic before they get their arms around it all. "I simply couldn't juggle all the new details at once," one frustrated worker confessed. "I felt like I was trying to nail Jell-O to a tree."

2. *Get closure on this conference.* The conference with the employee should close with a clear understanding of which parts of the job, if any, you'll take back and which ones will be left with your subordinate. In addition, make sure the two of you agree on the standards that must be met, and establish a timetable for following up on progress. This timetable is especially important because it keeps lines of communication open, provides a built-in rationale for making future contact, and ensures the person that he or she isn't being left to sink or swim.

The conference and its resulting closure speak well for you as a boss. You come across as a cool-headed coach and counselor instead of an impulsive dictator or a whip-cracking galleymaster. Your worker knows what is wrong and why and has an action list and perhaps a model to follow to bring the work up to standard by a specific deadline.

3. *Back up your words with action.* Monitor your employee's performance regularly, realizing that he or she may be anxious or defensive because of the circumstances. Show concern without oversupervising, and follow up with open-ended requests or questions such as, "Tell me how everything is going" and "Which problems should we discuss?"

Make an effort to praise improvement whenever praise is justified. Praise alleviates anxiety and confirms that the person is making progress.

4. *Delegate additional parts of the job as performance improves.* Any satellite duties that you took back can be redelegated as performance improves and the person gains confidence. Consider relaying these tasks piecemeal, however, so your employee can integrate them into the existing routine gradually. Passing them down all at once may trigger another round of confusion and frustration.

When you add a new segment of the job, explain its importance and emphasize how it relates to the work previously assigned. This technique helps the employee see the overall task both as a whole and as the sum of its parts—to see the forest as well as the trees.

(Well-man-
aged, inno-
vative or-
ganiza-
tions) . . .
give their
people the
right to be
wrong.

—LAUREL
CUTLER

DEVELOPING SKILL

Experienced supervisors realize that delegation is an acquired skill. Relaying work to subordinates successfully takes practice and the willingness to work with people who may have trouble handling an entire job all at once. Managers who are willing to help their employees over some early rough spots build a working bond that ensures that they, their subordinates, and the entire organization grow beyond yesterday's skills to master the challenges of tomorrow.

REVIEW AND REFLECT

How Do You Rate?

Rate yourself on each of the following qualities. Make a special note of those that you either lack or need to improve. Be honest!

DELEGATION SKILLS

	Yes	No	Need to Improve
a. I'm comfortable accepting the risks that go along with delegation.	_____	_____	_____
b. I believe I delegate about as much as I should.	_____	_____	_____
c. I understand and appreciate most of the benefits of delegation.	_____	_____	_____
d. I describe delegated duties clearly.	_____	_____	_____
e. I follow up and encourage feedback after making an assignment.	_____	_____	_____
f. I'm tolerant of honest mistakes when things go wrong.	_____	_____	_____

	Yes	No	Need to Improve
g. I analyze the task and the available employees carefully before choosing someone to dologate to.	_____	_____	_____
h. I know enough about the nature and abilities of my employees to make reasonably sound choices when I delegate.	_____	_____	_____
i. I'm willing to delegate to a relatively inexperienced worker if the task will expand the person's confidence, competence, and skills.	_____	_____	_____
j. I'm easily approached for advice or information when employees have problems with delegated assignments.	_____	_____	_____

What's Next?

Describe the specific, routine tasks you do that are good candidates for delegation. Name the most appropriate subordinate(s) you could delegate them to, the reasons for your choice, and steps to take to set the wheels in motion.

Task: _____

_____

Person to delegate to and why: _____

_____

_____

What should I do to begin?

1. _____

2. _____

3. _____

4. _____

Task: _____

_____

Person to delegate to and why: _____

_____

_____

What should I do to begin?

1. _____

2. _____

3. _____

4. _____

Task: _____

_____

Person to delegate to and why: _____

_____

_____

What should I do to begin?

1. _____

2. _____

3. _____

4. _____

CHAPTER 8

HIRING AND ORIENTING NEW EMPLOYEES

Managers who hire and orient new employees effectively enhance the success of their departments and organization many times over. These two activities are instrumental in maximizing productivity and morale and minimizing turnover. This chapter sets out the basic techniques and tips that will sharpen your ability to pick proficient new employees and help them get their feet on the ground once they're on the payroll.

HIRING

Identifying Applicants

Let's assume that the personnel department recruits candidates and accepts and files their applications. Part of your job is to select qualified applicants from the available pool when a vacancy occurs.

You and/or the personnel department should have prepared a specification for each job, summarizing the minimum education, training, experience, special skills, and other essentials an applicant must have in order to do the job satisfactorily. Analyze the job specification's requirements and compare them with information that candidates provided on the application. Those who are clearly unqualified may be disregarded at this point; those who appear to have the right qualifications may be called in for a personal interview.

Interviewing Guidelines

Productive interviews happen only through conscious effort. Get the most out of interviews by following these standard guidelines:

1. List the topics you want to discuss or areas that need to be clarified based on information on the application.
2. Pick a comfortable location free from telephone calls, drop-by visitors, and other interruptions.
3. Try to put the applicant at ease with some small talk. Be cordial and informal.
4. Answer the applicant's questions about the job and your organization.
5. Be objective. Guard against making positive or negative judgments based on an applicant's personality, appearance, or personal information. *Concentrate on assessing the applicant's qualifications for the job.*
6. Listen more than you talk. Nondirective or open-ended questions (those that can't be answered "yes" or "no") encourage applicants to express their true opinions and feelings.
7. Listen critically. Make a mental note of interview topics that elicited evasive, volatile, enthusiastic, inconsistent, emotional, or otherwise memorable responses.
8. Conclude the interview by thanking the applicant for his or her time and telling the person how long it will be before you'll make a decision. Don't leave the person hanging. Your courtesy may pay off in goodwill and the individual's willingness to reapply later if he or she is turned down for this job.
9. Record your impressions, responses to key questions, and information about the topics you wanted to cover in your notes immediately after the interview.

Interview Format

Whether you use a directive, nondirective, or combination interview depends on your experience, the amount of time you have for interviewing, and the nature of the job you're going to fill.

A *directive interview* follows a standardized list of questions. Although this format tends to be somewhat inflexible, it places you in firm control of the conversation and ensures that you'll cover all major topics in a minimum length of time. A directive interview is sometimes favored by inexperienced interviewers, but its checklist approach can make it sound like an interrogation to applicants. What's more, applicants won't have many chances to volunteer additional information that might affect your hiring decision.

A *nondirective interview* is extremely flexible: it uses open-ended questions instead of a cut-and-dried format. You begin with a general idea of the information you want from the applicant and phrase questions to create rapport, reveal attitudes, and elicit opinions and responses that may disclose more about an applicant's qualifications than a directive interview tends to do.

Conducting a nondirective interview takes experience. You must be able to steer the conversation back on course when applicants ramble off on a tangent. You'll also have to make sure that you cover all the topics that you meant to discuss when you compared the person's application against the job specifications.

A *combination interview* uses both directive and nondirective techniques, and many managers use it for that reason. For example, a directive format is handy for covering basic information on the application:

> "What specific types of heavy equipment are you qualified to operate?"
> "Why were you laid off by XYZ Inc.?"
> "Your application says you were unemployed from _____ to _____. Tell me what you did during that time."
> "Which desktop PC programs can you run?"
> "I see you're working toward your general equivalency diploma. When will you be finished?"

You can switch to a nondirective format to discuss and attempt to evaluate career goals, verbal communication skills, persuasiveness, dependability, temperament, ambition, self-motivation, and human relations skills—for example:

"Why do you want to work for our company?"

"How would you describe your ideal job?"

"I see that you've had three employers in the last two years. Why did you change jobs so often?"

"Why do you want to change jobs now?"

"What part of your previous job did you like or dislike the most? . . . Why?"

"If you finish an assignment early, how do you use the leftover time?"

"How would you react if you asked somebody in another department for information and he told you to get lost?"

"Can you give me an example of a memorable mistake you made in a former job? . . . What did you learn from that experience?"

"Describe your greatest strengths and weaknesses."

"Describe yourself the way you think your former boss would describe you."

"What do you see yourself doing three years from now?"

"How do you motivate yourself to do an unpleasant job?"

"What kind of people do you like to work with?"

"Do you think you work well as a member of a team? . . . Why [or why not]?"

Legal Concerns

Federal and state employment laws are designed to ensure that everyone has equal access and opportunity to jobs and promotions. They're specifically meant to protect racial and religious minorities, women, the disabled, and people age forty and over.

While claims of hiring discrimination are extremely hard to

prove, no one wants to get hauled into court. Unfortunately, there's no neat list of illegal questions. Even if you don't mean to discriminate, the implications of some questions that managers could ask within an employment interview context may prompt a court to declare them (and your organization) discriminatory. For example, asking if an applicant can work on weekends may seem innocent, but religious beliefs prohibit Orthodox Jews from traveling on Saturday.

Interview questions must be strictly job related. Avoid questioning applicants about:

- Race, ethnic background, or family history
- Language usually spoken at home
- Membership in ethnic clubs or organizations
- Marital status
- Birth control, family planning, children's ages, or child-care arrangements
- Spouse's occupation
- Sexual orientation or preferences
- Church attended; religious beliefs and practices
- Nature or extent of disabilities
- Medical history
- Age or birthdate
- Arrest record
- Wage attachments or garnishment
- Questions asked of one sex only (for example, asking only female applicants if they can type)

Perhaps the simplest guideline of all is to focus on interview questions and selection criteria that relate to the applicant's qualifications for and ability to perform the job you have to fill.

Perhaps the simplest guideline of all is to focus on interview questions and selection criteria that relate to the applicant's qualifications for and ability to perform the job you have to fill. If you do so, you'll be headed in the right direction.

ORIENTATION: WHERE DO THEY GO FROM HERE?

Have you ever been tossed into a job and left to sink or swim? If so, you know how important thorough orientation can be. When sound hiring decisions are followed by thorough orientation, turnover will be minimized and productivity and morale boosted. In addition, savvy managers cash in on the opportunity provided during orientation to regale new workers with all the positive aspects about the job, department, and organization while their enthusiasm is high.

Some organizations have highly detailed orientation procedures, including a checklist of orientation topics that managers are required to cover during the first several days and weeks. Others do not. If yours is one of the latter, here's how to help new employees get up to speed quickly and feel comfortable in their jobs and with their colleagues.

1. *Have the new employee fill out all payroll and personnel forms,* if the personnel department hasn't done so. Explain options about insurance coverage, income tax withholding, and other similar areas.

2. *Review each duty and responsibility listed on the employee's job description.* Emphasize that you may ask the person to do certain work that isn't specifically mentioned (unless such requests are prohibited by a union contract or other agreement). It's often important to clarify this so employees understand management's need for reasonable flexibility in making work assignments.

3. *Give the worker a copy of the employee handbook and related literature* covering such topics as company history, the insurance program, retirement benefits, credit union, tuition reimbursement, employee assistance program, employee suggestion program, and child-care assistance. Explain all relevant policies, procedures, and rules on appropriate workplace behavior, acceptable attire, affirmative action, timekeeping, promotions, pay raises, discipline, performance evaluation, vacations, holidays, sick leave, funeral leave, maternity leave, lateness and absenteeism, layoffs and recalls, break periods, lunchtime, overtime pay, and use of safety equipment. Answer all of the new worker's questions, contacting the personnel department if you need more information.

4. *Show how the new person's job relates to the other jobs in your department, how it affects the work of colleagues in related*

departments, and how your department integrates with other departments and with the entire facility. An organization chart can be very useful; it makes this information clear and easy to understand and gives the employee a model of how everything is supposed to fit.

5. *Take the newcomer on a walking tour of your department and surrounding areas.* Point out the location of break rooms, rest rooms, lockers, mail facilities, and copy machines. Introduce the person to everyone in your department and to coworkers in other departments whom he or she will work with frequently. As you do, share some personal information that may create rapport and help to break the ice ("Helen is a big fan of the Kansas City Chiefs"; "Joe is restoring a '76 Datsun 280-Z"; "Tim is president of the Lions Club"; "Stacey just got back from a vacation in Las Vegas.")

What you manage in business is people.

—HAROLD GENEEN

Assume the new worker will be feeling uncertain, confused, and somewhat frustrated, so make certain he or she feels free to ask you questions, and keep yourself accessible. Although orientation may be mostly your responsibility, you may want to use a "buddy system," matching up the new employee with an employee who knows the ropes. New workers are often more comfortable discussing questions or admitting ignorance to peers than to a supervisor. Make sure the experienced employee is committed to being a conscientious mentor and takes the responsibility seriously.

REVIEW AND REFLECT

True/False and Multiple Choice

Answer the true/false statements by placing a "T" or "F" in the space provided. Answer the multiple-choice questions by circling the number of the most correct answer.

a. _____ An interviewer should compare the application with the job specification after the interview is concluded.

b. _____ A directive interview gives the interviewer minimal control over the discussion.

c. _____ Questions asked in a nondirective interview should be able to be answered "yes" or "no."

d. _____ A combination interview would generally be considered an acceptable compromise between a directive and a nondirective interview.

e. _____ The applicant should talk more than the interviewer.

f. Which of the following interview formats is often preferred by inexperienced interviewers?
   1. exit interview
   2. stress interview
   3. directive interview
   4. nondirective interview

g. Which of the following interviews is often the most productive for gathering information on both basic information and intangible qualities?
   1. directive interview
   2. stress interview
   3. nondirective interview
   4. both 1 and 3

h. Which of the following is *not* recommended when conducting an employment interview?
   1. Compare the job specification against the application.
   2. Speak and act informally.
   3. Allow the applicant to ask questions about the job and the organization.
   4. Form opinions during the interview based on the applicant's personality, appearance, and personal information.

Put It in Focus

Indicate which of the following questions would be permissible to ask job applicants by placing a Y (for yes) or an N (for no) in front of each one.

a. _____ "Bernice, what made you decide to apply for a job here?"

b. _____ "Yoshi, how many of your family members have moved here from Japan so far?"

c. _____ "It sounds as if you have a very good job at Apex Industries. Why do you want to leave?"

d. _____ "Michelle, where do you want to be and what do you want to be doing ten years from now?"

e. _____ "I see you belong to the Sons of Norway. What offices have you held in that club?"

f. _____ "What would you do if you had to work closely with someone you didn't like?"

g. _____ "Have you ever had your pay garnished for unpaid bills, child support, or things like that?"

h. _____ "Elaine, how does your husband feel about your applying for a job that requires so much travel?"

i. _____ "Ms. Martinez, do you speak Spanish at home?"

j. _____ "George, what makes you think we should hire you?"

k. _____ "Will your child-care arrangements ensure that you can be here on time every day?"

l. _____ "Tell me at least two things that you're not very good at, and why."

m. _____ "Why have you had two jobs in the past eighteen months, Brent?"

n. _____ "I notice you're confined to a wheelchair, Alex. Are you sure you'd be able to do the type of work this job requires?

o. _____ "What kind of work suits you best?"

Brainstormer's Corner

Review your routine responsibilities for orienting new employees. List at least four specific ways you could improve how effectively or efficiently you carry out these duties. Then list at least three specific new actions you could take, *in addition to what's required by your job description,* to orient new workers more effectively.

IMPROVING ORIENTATION SKILLS

_____
_____
_____
_____
_____
_____
_____
_____
_____
_____

NEW WAYS TO ORIENT EMPLOYEES

_____
_____
_____
_____
_____
_____
_____
_____
_____
_____
_____

CHAPTER 9

MOTIVATING PEOPLE TO DO THEIR BEST

Motivation causes employees to invest more of themselves in their jobs than they're required to do. Motivated people reach beyond the boundaries of their job description and push the limits of their abilities not because they have to but because they want to. They go the extra mile to make sure that the people they serve, whether colleagues or customers, are fully satisfied. Motivated people not only do things right; they also do the right thing, and do it willingly.

You learned about hiring in the preceding chapter for a very good reason: Sound hiring makes motivating infinitely easier. Think about your own experience. Have you ever had a job you weren't compatible with, even though you were qualified to do it? The odds are that your boss had little success in motivating you to do more than absolutely necessary. If you start by selecting applicants who enjoy the basic character of the work they've been hired to do, your chances of motivating them to turn in above-average performance increase considerably. The feelings of qualified but "unmotivatable" employees are expressed by the bumper sticker that says, "I love my job. It's the work I hate."

ROLE MODELS

Effective motivation begins with you, because the enthusiasm and motivation you display toward your job is contagious. Workers tend to reflect their boss's traits, values, standards, and work habits. Managers who move forward on their own initiative are positive role models. Instead of cajoling, threatening, or cheerleading, they take command, lead by example, and demand as much from themselves as they do from their staff. Their motto might be, "Do as I say *and* as I do."

How can you be a positive role model? Let's start with the basics.

Make sure to give your employees their fair share of any praise that comes your way. In management, as in sports, it takes a team effort to bring home the trophy.

- Arrive at work on time.
- Be punctual with appointments.
- Return calls promptly.
- Respect and follow policies, procedures, and rules.
- Set challenging goals for yourself.
- Support strict quality standards.
- Put in longer hours and greater effort when necessary to honor your commitments to colleagues and customers.

Role models are loyal to their team. Demonstrate your loyalty by demanding recognition for your group's achievements and bringing those achievements to higher management's attention. Make sure to give your employees their fair share of any praise that comes your way. In management, as in sports, it takes a team effort to bring home the trophy.

MOTIVATIONAL THEORIES THAT WORK IN PRACTICE

Textbooks discuss many motivational theorists; two provide viewpoints that are especially relevant to new managers.

Douglas McGregor

McGregor tended to place managers into one of two categories: Theory X or Theory Y. According to McGregor, a Theory X boss tends to expect the worst from people. This person might say, "People are lazy; they can't be trusted;

they only work for money; they have to be supervised closely." A Theory Y boss tends to expect the best from others. This boss might say, "I believe people are basically ambitious and trustworthy. They want more from their jobs than a paycheck, and they don't need to have their managers breathing down their necks."

What level of performance are these two types of managers likely to get from their people? Usually the degree that they seem to expect. Since Theory X bosses expect the worst, why should their employees try to do better than average? There is little reason to exceed mediocrity if your boss has low expectations and a negative opinion of you. Theory Y bosses, by contrast, expect people to live up to their standards and may even ask employees to do more than they believe they're capable of. The results can be rewarding. If you select the best-qualified people and let them know you expect their best performance, they'll often respond by doing their darndest not to disappoint you.

Frederick Herzberg

Herzberg contended that motivation is affected by two sets of job-related factors. Maintenance factors are the basic things that workers believe they're entitled to, such as adequate pay, satisfactory working conditions, and competitive fringe benefits. People who don't receive these basics will be dissatisfied and may resign. Even if they do receive them, however, they aren't motivated. Who was ever motivated by fair treatment?

What does motivate people, according to Herzberg, is a chance to grow within the job and to be promoted. Praise for work well done and a basic liking for the work itself are additional motivational factors.

Herzberg's message to managers is to give employees the basic or maintenance factors that they expect (and will be dissatisfied without) and then load in as many factors as possible to provide satisfaction and foster motivation.

A MOTIVATOR'S TOOL KIT

When the chemistry is right between people and their jobs, various motivational tools may cause them to put their best efforts behind what they do. Each of these tools is in sync with McGregor's and Herzberg's theories of motivation.

Delegate Authority

Delegation, which you learned about in Chapter 7, can be a motivating force when it's applied at the right time, in the right place, to the right workers. In fact, it is one of the most powerful and meaningful ways that managers can express their faith and confidence in people. Symbolically delegation says, "I trust you," "I believe you'll do your best," and "I think you'll use sound judgment." All of this makes you a Theory Y manager according to McGregor.

Delegated authority also provides some of Herzberg's motivational factors. For example, authority gives workers an opportunity to grow within their jobs, test their own ideas, expand their skills and know-how, and gain experience that helps them become more confident, competent, and promotable. Delegation can be an exhilarating and highly motivating experience; giving people authority makes them feel important, respected, trusted, and valued.

Give Praise for Work Well Done

A well-deserved pat on the back at the right moment can be motivating. People know when they've exceeded expectations, and they hope their boss will recognize their accomplishments. Sincere praise and congratulations for outstanding performance stimulate some workers to increase their efforts to exceed their personal best.

Enlarge the Job

Full-scale job enlargement requires top-down management commitment and support. However, depending on your operations, authority, and budget, you might be able to enlarge some jobs under your control in a limited way and enhance your employees' performance accordingly.

Job enlargement changes a job's content and breadth to make it more meaningful. For example, instead of having workers assemble several parts, you could enlarge their jobs by having them build entire units, run quality assurance tests, repair any defects, and put their names on each unit before sending it on to the next department. Enlarged jobs are more satisfying; people feel gratified by the closure that comes from doing a comprehensive set of tasks from start to finish.

If you think that job enlargement requires a change in training and compensation, you're probably right. Workers who are given more responsibility must be trained to handle the additional tasks, and they'll rightfully expect to be paid for increased responsibility. For this reason, job enlargement may not fall entirely within the scope of your authority. The concept has outstanding motivational potential, however, and many·organizations have used it with excellent success.

Use Participative Management

This motivational tool can be used by any manager who decides to let employees have a greater voice in decisions that affect their jobs or the structure of the work itself.

Participative managers lead democratically, letting their people participate in relevant decisions. Many workers will be motivated to exercise more initiative and creativity because the boss will listen and respond to what they have to say.

Faced with the prospect of laying off employees to stay profitable in a recession, managers at a small glass manufacturing company took the situation to the rank and file. "We have to cut costs by X percent," they said. "The traditional way to do this is to lay off some of our people, but we don't want to do that if you can find another way. If you can recommend any workable way to cut costs as much as we need to, just tell us; we'll listen."

Workers met on their own time, discussed the problem, and finally suggested that everyone take a voluntary pay cut.

People don't change their behavior unless it makes a difference for them to do so.

—Fran Tarkenton

Although this meant less money for each of them, they knew they'd all keep their jobs, and the company would be able to show a profit. Management agreed, and the business survived without laying off a single person.

Rotate Jobs

Job rotation trains workers to perform several different jobs within their area so they can swap responsibilities and cover for each other when some are absent or on vacation. Job rotation obviously gives managers greater flexibility when making job assignments, but the technique has considerable motivation potential too. Workers who can do several jobs instead of just one may be more enthusiastic and motivated because of the variety and escaping the same daily grind.

The occupational agility that comes from job rotation makes people interchangeable parts in the best sense of the term. Knowing they can rotate among several jobs often prompts employees to invest more effort and zeal in what they do. There's also the motivating influence that comes with greater job security. People who can do several different tasks are more valuable than colleagues who know how to do one job only.

REVIEW AND REFLECT

How Do You Rate?

Rate yourself on each of the following qualities. Make a special note of those that you either lack or need to improve. Be honest!

ROLE MODELS AND MOTIVATION

	Yes	No	Need to Improve
a. I believe I'm a good role model for my employees in most respects.	___	___	___

	Yes	No	Need to Improve
b. I never bend the rules.	_____	_____	_____
c. I set challenging goals for myself.	_____	_____	_____
d. I do as much as I can to ensure that my staff gets the recognition it deserves.	_____	_____	_____
e. I generally fit the profile of a Theory Y boss according to Douglas McGregor.	_____	_____	_____
f. I assign work in ways that help my employees grow within their jobs and qualify for advancement.	_____	_____	_____
g. I think of delegation as a motivational tool.	_____	_____	_____
h. I praise good performance whenever I see it.	_____	_____	_____
i. I'm comfortable allowing my employees to help make decisions that affect them.	_____	_____	_____

Brainstormer's Corner

Review your subordinates' job descriptions and your own authority and budget discretion. Then answer the following questions.

1. Which of your employees' jobs could be enlarged without causing extensive retraining and major pay scale revisions?

_____

_____

2. Whose approval would you require to make or initiate these changes? _____

_____

3. How would you go about securing that approval? ___

_____

_____

4. Which jobs within your area are primary candidates for job rotation? _____

_____

_____

5. Whose approval would you require to begin the necessary cross-training? _____

_____

6. How would you deal with employees' concerns or objections? _____

_____

_____

7. Chances are that some of your employees are consistently unhappy in their present jobs. What can you do to help these workers identify the type of work they'd rather do? What specific actions might you take to help them become qualified for that work?

Name: _____

    To identify preferred work: _____

_____

_____

    Training plan: _____

_____

_____

Name: _____

    To identify preferred work: _____

_____

_____

    Training plan: _____

_____

_____

Name: _____

    To identify preferred work: _____

_____

_____

    Training plan: _____

_____

_____

Name: _____

    To identify preferred work: _____

_____

_____

    Training plan: _____

_____

_____

CHAPTER 10

APPRAISING PERFORMANCE

Employees need and usually want feedback about the quality of their work. Your ability to evaluate their performance objectively and constructively has a major impact on their success as well as yours.

FOUNDATION FOR APPRAISAL

If your company has a formal appraisal program, you must, of course, follow its guidelines in terms of timing (e.g., annual, semiannual, quarterly evaluations), rating system (e.g., numerical ratings or such designations as excellent, good, satisfactory, needs improvement), and the relationship of the evaluation to pay, promotion, training, and disciplinary decisions.

Whatever your company policies require, the following suggestions can make your appraisal process more effective.

Quantify Performance Goals If Possible

Quantified goals are objective goals; there is little debate about whether employees reached them—for example:

> "I plan to decrease customer complaints by at least 10 percent in the hardware department this year."
> "I'm going to cut scrap and rework by 15 percent this quarter."
> "I'm going to increase the number of claims processed by a minimum of 8 percent per month."

Expressing goals numerically instead of in vague or subjective terms helps to prevent positive or negative bias on your part and enables employees to focus their efforts and assess their own progress clearly and precisely.

Should You Keep a Diary?

Some managers use a diary to record significant incidents and specific examples of employees' performance that might otherwise slip their minds from one work period to the next. A record ensures that you'll collect information throughout the entire work period and produce a more complete and valid evaluation than if you relied on memory alone. Without a comprehensive record, your ratings may be slanted toward employees' most recent performance. (Workers, of course, may try to cash in on that oversight by suddenly shaping up several weeks before their regular evaluation is due.) A diary also accumulates most of the information you'll need to prepare evaluations in one place so you won't have to dig through files and round up material from several sources.

If you decide to keep a diary, a few words of caution are in order:

- Keep it in a safe location, preferably off the premises. If the record is saved on a computer disk, lock the file with a code that snoopers can't crack by trial and error. Don't use codes that others might figure out, such as your license tag or house number.
- Make sure to record positive information. If you don't make a conscious effort to include some "attaboys," your diary may deteriorate into a hit list of criticisms and mistakes.
- Purge older information once it becomes irrelevant so it won't affect your judgment about more recent performance.

Consider Self-Evaluation

Some managers ask employees to evaluate themselves as a preface to the formal review. In addition to being a constructive experience, this practice broadens the base of information you can use to prepare the official evaluation.

When subordinates evaluate themselves, they'll think critically about their progress and achievements. In addition, they're required to view their performance from your perspective as well as their own. Self-evaluation gives them an opportunity to inform you of accomplishments, recognition, and problems you might be unaware of.

As far as you're concerned, self-evaluation offers several benefits:

- It creates a new channel of communication.
- You come across as a participative manager who both encourages and expects employees to take an active role in the appraisal process.
- Self-evaluation helps you confirm or modify your opinions of your people's performance in the light of information provided by them.

Subordinates may abuse or be misled by a self-evaluation policy, however, unless you set at least two ground rules:

1. Require them to supply quantified (or at least verifiable) support for their own ratings. If you don't, some employees may give themselves a much higher rating than they really deserve. Refuse to accept what they say about themselves at face value. If they can't justify their own ratings, you'll be obliged to lower their inflated opinions with evidence of your own.

2. Clarify that this opportunity is a privilege, not a right. Their self-evaluation is just one of the sources you may use to make the formal appraisal more thorough and accurate.

Nip Pending Problems in the Bud

One of the best ways to help your staff earn justifiably high performance reviews is to tell them about unacceptable behavior or performance without delay. This gives them the opportunity to correct problems before they end up on the record. For example, a worker who starts returning late from lunch regularly or handing in sloppy work should be informed of the problem and its potential impact on the annual review. This practice is better than letting the situation drag on for several months, dropping the bomb at evaluation time, and having the upset person ask, "Why didn't you mention this sooner?"

PITFALLS OF PERFORMANCE APPRAISALS

Performance appraisals are subject to several hazards, but you can navigate around them successfully once you know what they are.

• *The halo effect and negative impressions.* In performance appraisals, as in hiring, managers have to guard against forming positive or negative opinions based on personality traits or personal appearance. *Concentrate on evaluating how well the employee met clear-cut performance goals.* That's the key issue here.

• *Leniency.* Some managers tend to be permissive because they feel awkward or embarrassed about discussing performance deficiencies with workers. Although these feelings are understandable, your responsibility to level with substandard performers and counsel them about improving comes with the management territory.

Sooner or later, everyone suffers from a lenient appraisal. The organization doesn't get a fair return on its investment in these low performers. Employees, who may know full well that they're not working up to par, can lose respect for a boss who seems to be too wimpy to confront them. Employees also may get a false sense of security. Imagine their shock the first time they're rated by an up-front manager who knows they're slacking off and tells them so.

• *Central tendency.* This pitfall, a second cousin of leniency, is the inclination to rate everyone's performance as acceptable. Central tendency does an injustice to outstanding performers, however, because they're denied the recognition and praise they deserve. At the same time, their underachieving coworkers are allowed to slide by with acceptable ratings.

• *Focus on recent behavior.* Recent behavior is easiest to recall, but it tells only part of the story. Your evaluation should assess performance for the entire period of time since the last rating, not just recent events or achievements.

THE EVALUATION CONFERENCE

Although some managers consider evaluation interviews a necessary evil, the information exchanged during this discussion can be extremely important to your employees. Most of us are anxious to know how our boss thinks we're doing, so give this meeting the respect and effort it deserves.

Planning the Conference

Set a mutually convenient date and time. Avoid scheduling the meeting on a birthday, wedding anniversary, Friday, or just before or after the worker's vacation. This gives too much time for anxiety to build. People are in a better position to address their shortcomings when they know they can attack them first thing in the morning. Then tell the employee what you're going to discuss so he or she arrives emotionally prepared.

Review the person's job description and records (including the diary and self-evaluation material, if used). Then reflect on the employee's duties and responsibilities, major projects completed or pending, agreed-upon goals for the past work period, training, experience, special skills, and such qualities as job knowledge, overall work quality, planning and organizing skill, initiative, ability to work well with colleagues, problem-solving ability, and other performance-based attributes.

To ensure privacy during your conference, hold all telephone calls or retreat to a quiet location where the two of you won't be interrupted. Don't postpone or reschedule a conference unless it's absolutely necessary. Putting it off diminishes its importance and frustrates employees who naturally want to get it over with.

Honing Your Techniques

Some managers take a "criticism sandwich" approach: opening the interview by praising outstanding accomplishments and qualities, discussing areas that need improvement and precise, tangible actions that the employee can take to correct or elevate performance in those areas, and closing the meeting with a restatement of strong points. Bracketing problems or weak spots with positive feedback helps prevent employees from becoming overwhelmed by their deficiencies and blowing them out of proportion.

Effective performance appraisers are coaches, counselors, and collaborators. They're committed to helping people elevate their performance and reach their true potential in the future.

It's vital to criticize constructively. After pointing out areas where employees fell short of their goals or need to improve, you must tell them what specifically they can do to resolve or eliminate the difficulty. Avoid vague and subjective phrases like "You seem," "It appears," or "I believe" and referring to the person's "attitude" (which cannot be quantified or nailed down). Support your evaluation by citing incidents, dates, times, and objective evidence of both strong and weak performance.

Effective performance appraisers are coaches, counselors, and collaborators. They're committed to helping people elevate their performance and reach their true potential in the future.

Never compare peers with each other. Comparing two subordinates by name ("You should try to be more like Smedley; she has excellent initiative and is the best performer in your group") can cause trouble. Singling out one person as a role model for the rest creates resentment toward the high achiever. Instead, concentrate on how well the person you're evaluating met performance goals that were established at the beginning of the work period.

BEYOND APPRAISAL

Performance appraisals are guidelines to success. They confirm strengths, reveal shortcomings, and highlight employees' needs for additional experience and training.

No evaluation is complete without guidance and direction that will help employees strengthen notable weaknesses and pursue excellence in areas they are strong in. A complete appraisal should include a program of personal development activities, created and agreed upon by both you and your employee, that will correct weaknesses and develop or enhance future performance. These activities may include, for example, registering workers in appropriate in-house courses or seminars and encouraging them to enroll in programs offered by the public school system, trade schools, and community colleges. The effort you invest in developing outstanding subordinates will pay dividends in the performance of your overall department and add to the reputation and success of everyone involved.

> **Judge a tree from its fruit; not from the leaves.**
>
> **—EURIPIDES**

REVIEW AND REFLECT

How Do You Rate?

Rate each of the following factors. Make a special note of those that you do not have or believe you should obtain or improve. Be honest!

EVALUATING EMPLOYEES' PERFORMANCE

	Yes	No	Need to Improve or Obtain
a. I have a job description for each position that reports to me.	_____	_____	_____

	Yes	No	Need to Improve or Obtain
b. I can get quantified or verifiable goals for each position.	_____	_____	_____
c. I have records that provide evidence of each person's accomplishments.	_____	_____	_____
d. I have access to records that help me decide what type of training and development activities would be appropriate for each person.	_____	_____	_____
e. I believe I should create a performance diary for the people who report to me.	_____	_____	_____
f. Self-evaluation would be useful and appropriate for gathering information on my employees' performance.	_____	_____	_____
g. I don't warn employees about their unacceptable behavior or performance as promptly or frankly as I should.	_____	_____	_____
h. I tend to draw unjustified opinions about my staff based on their personal appearance and/or personalities.	_____	_____	_____
i. I'm more concerned about my staff's liking me than I am about informing them of areas where they need to improve.	_____	_____	_____
j. I tend to evaluate my employees over the entire work period instead of the past few weeks or months.	_____	_____	_____

(continues)

	Yes	No	Need to Improve or Obtain
k. I'm well informed about the resources my organization and the community offer to help employees correct and improve performance deficiencies.	_____	_____	_____
l. I encourage employees to obtain the training they need to correct performance problems and develop their full potential.	_____	_____	_____

What's Next?

Describe specific actions you can take to obtain missing information noted in How Do You Rate? or to develop or improve the traits and qualities that will enable you to appraise your employees' performance effectively.

IMPROVING MY EVALUATION TECHNIQUES

_____

_____

_____

_____

_____

CHAPTER 11

DISCIPLINE AND TERMINATION

Despite how carefully you apply the techniques you've learned so far in *The Successful New Manager,* you'll probably have to discipline and terminate employees sooner or later. Discipline and termination are two of the most unwelcome tasks that managers must do, but they come with the territory. As one major chemical company puts it, "Supervisors are rated on their willingness to assume and discharge the functions of management. [Discipline and termination are] functions of management." The information in this chapter will help you carry out these functions effectively and minimize their inherent stress and conflict.

DISCIPLINE

You've already learned about several practices that minimize the need for discipline: careful hiring, detailed and thorough orientation, effective leadership, and informing employees of unacceptable performance or behavior as soon as possible. Unfortunately, these measures cannot ensure that everyone will do what's required of them voluntarily or display appropriate conduct on the job.

Managers who discipline employees have been aptly compared to a hot stove. They should follow the hot stove rule:

1. Provide warning. (A hot stove sizzles before it burns.)
2. Act promptly. (A hot stove doesn't wait to respond.)
3. Be consistent. (A hot stove always burns.)

4. Make the penalty fit the offense. (A hot stove burns by degrees.)
5. Be impartial. (A hot stove burns everyone.)
6. Make no apology. (A hot stove doesn't say, "I'm sorry.")
7. Behave unemotionally. (A hot stove doesn't get upset or lose control.)

Stress Penalty, Not Punishment

Punishment carries a hint of vindictiveness. A penalty, on the other hand, is a cost that your organization requires errant workers to pay for the damage that their unacceptable behavior does to their department, their work team, or the overall organization. That damage may be lost time, endangering or obstructing the work of colleagues, offending customers, increasing scrap and rework, decreasing productivity, or physical destruction of equipment or facilities.

Discipline should be corrective and forward-looking. You hope the penalty a disciplined employee must pay will cause that person to display appropriate conduct in the future.

Discipline should be corrective and forward-looking. You hope the penalty a disciplined employee must pay will cause that person to display appropriate conduct in the future.

Be Fair But Firm

No matter how well disposed you might be toward the offender, you're obliged to be a hot stove manager when employees break the rules. Looking the other way or postponing your response will be interpreted as weakness or bias by the people you supervise. They may feel contemptuous toward you and hostile toward the employee whom you let off lightly.

Make policy the scapegoat for your disciplinary action—which indeed it is. As a member of management, you're obligated to carry out all the policies that pertain to your job. Implying that you have discretion in the matter makes you a target for the disciplined employee's anger.

Don't call attention to yourself with phrases such as, "I don't understand why . . . ," "I have no alternative . . . ," "I'm required to . . . ," or "I simply can't . . ." They make you a lighting rod for the person's hostility. Instead, use neutral expressions such as, "Policy requires that . . . ," "Work rules will not permit . . . ," and "The company cannot allow . . ."

Go by the Book

When a disciplinary problem occurs, consult your organization's disciplinary policy and procedure, and follow it precisely. If there is any ambiguity, ask your supervisor or a higher authority for direction.

It's always a good idea to inform your supervisor of the action you intend to take and get a personal endorsement. This helps to ensure that your decision won't be reversed if the employee files a grievance.

Your action may also be affected by precedent. If the issue isn't cut and dried, check disciplinary records or ask a higher authority to see if a similar case has occurred in the past and how it was handled. If there is no precedent, act carefully. Your response to this offense may set a precedent for future managers to follow. In any event, exercise the very best judgment you can summon.

Gather the Evidence

Most organizations consider employees innocent until proved guilty, so you must supply proof of the alleged violation. You'll look foolish if you go off half-cocked, overreact, or make vague allegations that fall apart under scrutiny.

Assemble documented evidence and/or reliable testimony about the employee's infraction from witnesses who will confirm that the incident took place. This material can be critical to your case if you're called on to defend yourself to higher management or in an arbitration hearing.

Use Progressive Discipline

Progressive discipline, a universal practice today, typically starts with an oral reprimand and policy restatement for minor offenses and escalates to more severe action depending on the gravity and frequency of the infraction.

Critical offenses justify immediate discharge. The employee will be suspended for no longer than three workdays while management investigates the incident. If circumstances do not excuse the employee's actions, the employee will be terminated without notice. Some examples of critical offenses are:

- Theft or dishonesty
- Assaulting, threatening, or intimidating customers or coworkers
- Willful damage of company property
- Unauthorized possession of weapons or explosives on company premises
- Possessing, consuming, or being under the influence of intoxicants, narcotics, or nonprescribed barbiturates on company premises
- Being absent for three consecutive scheduled workdays without proper notification or five one-day unexcused absences without notification in any twelve-month period
- Altering his or her time card or the time card of another employee

Major offenses are less serious than critical offenses but also require first offenders to be suspended for no more than three workdays. A second major offense will result in discharge. Some examples are:

- Committing two serious offenses within six months
- Violating safety rules that could cause harm or injury to customers or employees or major damage to equipment
- Harassing a coworker or customer
- Gambling on company premises

Serious offenses require the manager to place a written warning in the employee's personnel file. A second serious offense will result in suspension, and a third will result in discharge. Some examples are:

- Failure to use safety devices or equipment or to comply with safety precautions
- Smoking in restricted areas
- Work performance that does not meet established standards (such as misuse of time and loitering)
- Repeated or continued minor offenses (more than three in any three-month period)
- Use of vile, intemperate, or abusive language
- Removal of company property from the premises without written authorization
- Interference with or purposeful distraction of another employee's job performance

Minor offenses, finally, are relatively insignificant breaches of policies or rules that can be corrected without serious disciplinary measures. Offenders receive an oral reprimand for the first offense, a written warning for the second, suspension for the third, and discharge for the fourth. Some examples are:

- Unexcused tardiness
- Excessive break time
- Failure to observe a supervisor's instructions
- Attendance to personal business on company time
- Disorderly, loud, or unruly conduct
- Minor damage to company property

If no further disciplinary action is required within one year of a written warning, the warning is removed from the employee's file, and the disciplinary cycle starts over.

The Disciplinary Conference

A disciplinary conference is second only to a termination interview in its volatility. Since no two situations or workers are identical, there is no seamless set of guidelines for what you should say and do. Following are some general recommendations based on common sense, prudence, insight, and empathy:

1. Evaluate the circumstances surrounding the incident. For example, did the offender understand that a policy or rule was violated? Does the situation tend to encourage infraction (e.g., if your organization gives employees five unexcused absences each year, you can be pretty sure they'll take advantage of them). Might inadequate orientation, training, or supervision have contributed to the problem? Situations that seem to be causing repeat violations should be called to higher management's attention.

2. Review evidence that confirms the offense and can be used to justify your action—for example, production records, time sheets, samples of unacceptable work, or testimony from witnesses. Be sure to provide dates, times, and places.

3. Follow proper protocol:

- Meet privately, so your remarks won't be overheard.
- Provide seating. Emotions are less likely to escalate as long as at least one of you is sitting down.
- Maintain steady eye contact.
- Outline the facts of the matter calmly and clearly.
- Avoid physical contact. Even placing a conciliatory hand on someone's shoulder could lead to a charge of sexual harassment or physical assault.

4. Criticize the conduct, not the person. The message you send should be, "You're not an unacceptable person, but your behavior was unacceptable. It violated the rules of our organization, and it must change."

5. Ask the employee to explain why he or she committed the offense. An explanation cannot excuse what happened, but at least you've listened to the worker's side of the story.

6. Don't allow the discussion to wander off on personalities, speculation, unfounded allegations, or other red-herring issues. Stick to the facts.

7. Define and provide examples of acceptable performance. Clarify what the employee must do to resolve the problem permanently.

8. Be constructive. Work toward correcting, strengthening, and improving future conduct, not punishing prior conduct or "getting even."

9. Inform the offender of the steps that must be taken now and those that may be required later according to your organization's disciplinary procedure. Make sure the person understands that these steps must be followed without fail.

10. Conclude the conference by assuring the employee that you're available to answer any questions about what constitutes acceptable behavior. Express your confidence in the person's ability to resolve the problem permanently and successfully.

11. Make an informal record of the conference for your own files while the experience is fresh in your mind. Summarize your comments, the employee's responses, and other relevant information that might be important if the person files a grievance or doesn't take the necessary action.

TERMINATION

Working with people is difficult, but not impossible.

—PETER DRUCKER

If discipline is unpleasant for managers, then termination is downright repulsive. Terminating employees is the most stressful and unpleasant task that managers face, but virtually everyone has to deal with it sooner or later.

Most of the guidelines that relate to discipline apply to terminations too: be fair but firm, follow policy and procedure precisely, and gather indisputable evidence of the conduct that makes the termination necessary. Once you've completed each step in your organization's disciplinary procedure, or if the offense calls for immediate termination, then you've reached the end of the line.

Holding the Termination Interview

The termination interview is a classic no-win situation. The employee is going to be fired, and you've got to do it. About all you can do is try to make the best of a bad situation:

1. Review your records to refresh your memory on the issues, events, and conferences that led up to and justify this climax. Confirm that policy was followed to the letter.

2. Inform your boss before you act. If the employee appeals your decision to a higher level, your supervisor may have to discuss and defend your action.

3. Some organizations encourage managers to rehearse the termination interview with a human resources department employee first. If yours has such a program, use it. Role-playing the interview helps you refine your comments, clarify your thinking, anticipate the person's reaction, and prepare yourself for what's ahead.

4. Notify the proper people, including your supervisor and the security department, if you believe the terminated employee may threaten or commit bodily harm. Some employees turn violent, and even homicidal, when terminated.

5. As with discipline, make the employee's conduct and your organization's policy responsible for the termination. References to yourself make you a target for hostility.

6. Deal in facts. Don't let the interview deteriorate into an argument about personality differences or a plea for leniency ("This will destroy my career," "I tried my best but you don't like me," "I have a large family to support"). By definition, offenses that require termination have gone too far to salvage. A clean break is better than a bad tear.

7. Plan the interview so it won't fall on Friday, after the employee returns from vacation, or on the person's birthday or anniversary. The experience of being discharged is devastating enough as it is.

8. Try to limit the interview to no more than ten minutes. Hold the meeting away from your office; it's easier to conclude the discussion that way.

9. Deliver the news clearly and unemotionally.

10. Follow the same protocol suggested for disciplinary interviews. Handling terminations firmly, fairly, and gracefully improves your reputation with everyone else who works for you.

11. Collect the employee's identification card, name

badge, vehicle and office keys, confidential files, and company property such as a laptop computer, product samples, selling aids, and instruments or materials that the person may have used off the premises. If the person has access to computer files, cancel the password or access code immediately.

What Happens Afterward?

Traditional doctrines such as *employment at will* and *firing for just cause* have been turned upside-down by recent court decisions. The American Civil Liberties Union reports that the average jury verdict in wrongful termination lawsuits now exceeds $500,000. That's ample reason to handle terminations as smoothly and skillfully as possible.

A paper trail that confirms that everything was handled correctly and by the book can be vital to your organization's defense if an employee takes legal action. File all the material that you accumulated on the incident in a safe place and hope you won't need it.

Don't discuss any aspects of the termination or the worker's performance or conduct with other employees or prospective employers. A manager who states or even implies anything negative about a former employee to a prospective employer may be flirting with a lawsuit, and the costs of defense can be enormous. Fired employees have successfully sued former employers on such grounds as defamation of character, slander, intentionally inflicting emotional distress, invasion of privacy, and even "abusive discharge."

REVIEW AND REFLECT

True/False and Multiple Choice

Answer the true/false statements by placing a "T" or "F" in the space provided. Answer the multiple-choice questions by circling the number of the best answer.

a. ____ According to the hot stove rule, managers should vary the penalty to fit the offense.

b. ____ Managers should apologize for the fact that disciplinary action is necessary.

c. ____ Disciplinary action should be both impartial and impersonal.

d. The hot stove rule suggests that managers should:
1. Not conceal their anger when disciplining employees.
2. Let the discipline come as a surprise to the employee.
3. Refuse to let personal feelings affect disciplinary action.
4. all of the above

e. ____ The employment and orientation process have little, if any, impact on employee discipline.

f. When someone with an excellent work record violates a work rule, a manager should:
1. Ignore the first offense and give the person a second chance.
2. Explain to the person's coworkers why the situation was overlooked.
3. Penalize an employee whom the manager personally likes more severely to avoid charges of favoritism.
4. none of the above

g. ____ A manager should make policy and the employee's behavior responsible for disciplinary action.

h. ____ Managers should show empathy by implying that they have discretion in how they handle disciplinary issues.

i. Which of the following comments is most appropriate in a disciplinary interview?
1. "I don't think I have any other choice."
2. "Policy won't permit that kind of behavior."
3. "I'm sorry this has to happen."
4. "I want you to promise you'll shape up if I let you off this time."

j. The first thing to do when a disciplinary problem occurs is to:
    1. Consult your organization's disciplinary policy and procedure.
    2. Inform your supervisor.
    3. Reprimand the employee immediately, because you can always apologize if you were wrong.
    4. Take immediate action; then ask your supervisor to support what you did.

k. _____ A precedent to disciplinary action is relatively unimportant, because every employee is different.

l. _____ Most organizations consider employees innocent until proved guilty.

m. "Progressive discipline" refers to the fact that:
    1. Supervisors should take severe action when an offense occurs and apply progressively lighter penalties as the employee's conduct improves.
    2. Discipline should start with an oral reprimand for minor infractions and escalate to more severe action if the employee repeats the behavior.
    3. Progressively lighter penalties should be applied to employees who work in high-pressure jobs.
    4. Progressive organizations let the disciplined employees themselves decide which penalty will be applied.

n. _____ Disciplinary action should stress penalty, not punishment.

o. _____ Managers who must frequently discipline employees for violating the same work rule should ask higher management to review the nature or language of the rule itself.

p. Which of the following is *not* recommended in a disciplinary interview?
    1. Placing your hand on the employee's arm as a reassuring gesture
    2. Holding the interview in a private location

3. A willingness to admit that differences in your backgrounds or personalities may have affected your decision
4. 1 and 3

q. ＿＿ A manager should clarify why an employee's behavior required disciplinary action but make the employee find a way to correct it.

r. ＿＿ Disciplinary action should focus on previous rather than future conduct.

s. ＿＿ The guidelines that apply to disciplinary action are also appropriate for terminations.

t. ＿＿ You should inform your boss before terminating an employee, not after.

u. ＿＿ Rehearsing a termination interview with a third party is a waste of time.

v. Which of the following is most true about a termination interview?
1. It should be limited to no more than approximately ten minutes.
2. It should be held in the manager's office rather than elsewhere.
3. It should be held on a date such as the employee's birthday so he or she will remember the seriousness of the experience.
4. Its conduct will have little or no effect on how other subordinates feel toward the manager.

w. A manager should candidly discuss a former employee's termination, work habits, and overall performance with which of the following?
1. The employee's former coworkers
2. Prospective employers with whom the person has applied for a job
3. Members of the news media who may inquire about the incident
4. none of the above

Put It in Focus

Based on the chapter examples, indicate which of the following would tend to be categorized as critical, major, serious, or minor offenses by placing C, MA, S, or MI, respectively, in the space provided.

a. ____ Deleting files from a coworker's computer as a practical joke.

b. ____ Heckling coworkers about their nationality and ethnic background.

c. ____ Working bareheaded in a hard-hat area.

d. ____ Carrying a .38 automatic in an ankle holster.

e. ____ Making personal telephone calls during working hours.

f. ____ Using threats or abusive language to intimidate coworkers.

g. ____ Playing poker in the employees' break room.

h. ____ Infecting coworkers' computers with a virus that made their monitors display data upside down.

i. ____ Lifting heavy objects without wearing a back support.

j. ____ Returning five minutes late from work breaks regularly.

k. ____ Cursing at coworkers or subordinates.

l. ____ Informing a customer that an order that is lost in the warehouse had been shipped two days ago.

m. ____ Disorderly conduct on the premises.

n. ____ Sexual harassment.

o. ____ Keeping a pint of whiskey in the employees' locker room.

CHAPTER 12

COMMUNICATING FOR SUCCESS

Communication could be defined as transferring meaning. Sounds easy, doesn't it? You probably know from your own experience, though, that getting a message across to somebody else can be a lot harder than it seems.

BARRIERS TO SUCCESS

Successful communication can be torpedoed by several mental and verbal barriers. Recognizing them is the first step toward improving your person-to-person communication skills.

Inference-Observation Confusion

This happens when you infer more than you've actually seen (or heard) about a situation. For example, a superintendent ordered a man who was walking through a construction site to get a hard hat. When the fellow laughed and kept on going, the manager flew into a rage and told him he was suspended for three days for breaking a safety rule. "Take a hike, you idiot," the guy said. "I'm just cutting through here on my way to the store!"

Dealing with inference-observation confusion requires self-control. The difference between what you *know* and what you're merely *assuming* can be critical in some situations. Act on facts; refuse to jump to conclusions or shoot from the hip.

Allness

People who fall prey to this barrier assume that they know everything important about a subject. Bad mistake! Someone once said, "For every complex problem there's a simple answer, and it's wrong." Beware of oversimplifying an issue or assuming you're an expert just because you have had some experience with it. If you find yourself saying that you "know all about" the jobs your people do because you came up through the ranks, you may be wrong. Changing technology and techniques may have made your once-expert knowledge obsolete.

Indiscrimination

Indiscrimination causes managers to be so preoccupied with similarities that they ignore important differences. They may fail to discriminate, for example, among the unique ideas or approaches that each employee brings to the job; the kinds of work experience or development opportunities that motivate certain workers; or specific customers' needs and expectations. Victims of indiscrimination tend to view many situations as routine, treat people as cookie-cutter clones of each other, and take a by-the-numbers approach to solving problems. A manager who says, "People are the same everywhere you go," is a potential victim of indiscrimination.

Polarization

This barrier exists when you assume there is no middle ground between two extremes. Polarization sometimes occurs in the early stages of union-management negotiations: management may claim that labor's demands are outrageous and the company simply cannot afford them, while union negotiators declare that members won't accept a penny less than what they've asked for. As negotiations proceed, however, both sides tend to discover that there's some room for compromise between these either-or extremes.

Don't be guilty of giving or accepting take-it-or-leave-it choices. Negotiation is possible in most situations. If you want to avoid the barrier of polarization, be willing to discuss and compromise on areas where you and the other party disagree.

Frozen Evaluation

Here you form an opinion, freeze it in time, and assume that the condition or situation will never change. Saying that "you can't teach an old dog new tricks" or considering someone you hired inexperienced (although you may have hired the person two years ago) means you're a frozen evaluator.

Time changes all the circumstances and people who affect your job. Dating a situation or event by asking exactly when it happened, how much time has passed, and which conditions may have changed since then can give you a very different perspective.

Pointing and Associating

Pointing labels things, and those labels may call up positive or negative associations. Such associations are often stereotypes that may be inaccurate or confusing. Read the following list of words and ask what associations each one has for you:

Jock	Government officials
Nerd	Gay
Radical	Liberal
Politician	Lawyer
Laborer	Executive
Wall Street sources	Activist
Redneck	Yuppie

Words themselves can create prejudicial associations, depending on what they point your thoughts toward. This condition has encouraged the growth of doublespeak, jargon, and "politically correct" gobbledygook that dulls the edge of clarity:

- An "antipersonnel weapon" is one that kills people.
- Someone may be "dehired" instead of fired.
- Companies have recently "downsized," "rightsized," or made a "skill-mix adjustment" or "chemistry change" instead of laying off employees.
- Hospitals have reported "negative patient care outcomes" instead of deaths and "nonfacile manipulation of a newborn" when a clumsy nurse drops an infant on the delivery room floor.
- Insurance salespeople often call funeral and burial expenses "final costs" that must be paid after you "expire" or "transition" (die).
- There are no bad drivers working for one large parcel-delivery company. Management calls them the "least best."

If you want to test your susceptibility to pointing and associating, just ask yourself, "Which weighs more, a pound of lead or a pound of feathers?"

Your Status or Position

Have you ever glossed over a problem when you had to tell your boss about it? If so, you can appreciate how formal position can erect a communication barrier. The more formal position and status that people have in an organization, the more others may tend to tell them half-truths or what they think they want to hear.

Keep yourself approachable. Your subordinates must feel free to tell you the whole story without fear of being handed their heads.

Managers at every level must work hard to convince their people that they won't shoot messengers who bring bad news. Keep yourself approachable. Your subordinates must feel free to tell you the whole story without fear of being handed their heads.

SPEAKING VERSUS WRITING

Now that you can identify several major communication barriers, let's deal with some message mechanics. When should you send a message verbally, and when should you put it in writing? Your choice will be affected in part by how much time you have, how important the message is, the attitude and nature of your intended receiver(s), and whether you should keep a permanent record.

You may want to send a message verbally instead of putting it in writing when:

- You want immediate and direct feedback from the receiver. Speaking face to face permits you to ask questions, confirm the other person's understanding, and provide clarification.
- You don't want a written record. If writing will commit you too firmly to a course of action and take away your options or flexibility, you may not want to create documents that could come back to haunt you.
- There's not enough time to put something down on paper.
- Delivering the message in person will increase its impact or urgency.

You may want to put what you have to say in writing, however, if:

- Several people must act on the same instructions.
- There are regulatory, legal, or contractual requirements involved.
- You want to take a formal position on the matter, clarify an opinion, or dispel a rumor.
- You want to provide a precise set of instructions.
- The recipient has a history of disregarding or forgetting verbal instructions.

GIVING DIRECTIVES

There's more to directing than just telling people what you want them to do. To make your intentions known, you should:

- Be clear and definite about what you want done.
- Provide reasons when appropriate so employees can

respond intelligently and place this new directive in priority with your earlier ones.

- Demonstrate or illustrate the results you expect if employees are in doubt.
- Provide enough details to eliminate ambiguity or confusion.
- Verify that the directive is within policy and the employee's job description if the person expresses concern or reluctance.
- Assign a deadline if necessary.
- Respect employees' dignity. Don't talk down to them, treat them like robots, or overemphasize your formal authority.
- Encourage employees to ask questions about any part of the assignment and about problems that may arise after the job gets under way.

You can choose one of four formats, depending on the circumstances:

1. A *suggestion* is the least forceful type of directive. An employee may respond to a suggestion ("Why don't you try to get this order packed and shipped by Thursday morning?") if he or she is perceptive and responsive enough to realize that it should be taken to heart because it comes from you, the manager.

2. A *request* is more direct than a suggestion. You pointedly ask someone to do the job ("Will you see to it that this order is packed and shipped by Thursday morning?"). Requests are usually forceful enough to get your point across.

3. A *command* or *direct order* may be required in emergencies, when time is short, if workers are lazy or indifferent, or when you're assigning unpleasant work ("Jack, even though this order may be awkward to pack and ship, I want you to get it out by Thursday morning. Do you understand?"). Because of their dictatorial nature, commands should be used sparingly.

4. A *call for volunteers* may be fitting if the job is unusual or unpleasant and several employees are equally qualified and

eligible to do it ("We have to get this order packed and shipped by Thursday morning. I'd like one volunteer to get on it right away"). If no one volunteers, you'll have to resort to a request and maybe even a direct order.

LISTENING TIPS

Listening is hearing with a purpose. When you sharpen your listening skills, you can do more in less time, compliment and flatter others with your attention and interest, and eliminate mistakes caused by receiving incorrect or incomplete information.

Here are several basic tips that can make you a more efficient and effective listener:

- *Listen positively*. Try to learn something from what the speaker says.
- *Listen with a sensitive ear*. Empathize with the speaker. Don't assume that he or she understands your problem or point of view.
- *Evaluate and analyze what you hear*. Challenge the speaker's comments. Are they logical? Does the speaker supply credible support for them? Do they make sense? Distinguish between "nice to know" and "need to know" information.
- *React to what you hear*. Ask questions; summarize main points silently or repeat them back to the speaker; compare, contrast, and draw analogies.
- *Adjust to the speaker*. Get in tune with the person's gestures, facial expressions, pauses, secondary remarks, humorous quips, and rate of speech. Don't listen at one pace to what's being said at another.

BASIC BUSINESS WRITING TIPS

Everything you write says something about yourself as well as your subject. Expect others to judge you by the quality of your writing, because that's often all they have to go on.

David J. Buerger of Santa Clara University observed, "[With the advent of electronic mail], managers send and receive messages on a one-to-one basis. Now that secretaries don't fix their sloppy writing, the whole world wonders how they passed English 1A."

Outline, Incubate, and Edit

Outlining helps you to organize main points, supporting facts, and examples logically and to write your first draft quickly and easily.

Let your first draft *incubate* for a day or so while you reflect on how you might improve it.

Test for clarity as you *edit* with such questions as:

> "What do I really want to say?"
> "What sounds ambiguous, vague, or confusing?"
> "What questions have I left unanswered?"

Ask yourself how you'd explain the subject to your spouse, a new trainee, or someone else who knew nothing about it.

Editing should also eliminate clichés, unnecessary jargon, and overused words and phrases. Develop fresh expressions, new comparisons, and original examples that will add flair and style to your writing. These things don't happen automatically. "Learning to write is easy," said sportswriter Red Smith. "All you do is sit down at a typewriter and open a vein."

Avoid unsupportable claims or broad generalizations, such as "It's common knowledge . . ." or "Most people . . ." Provide references for statistics and other data to give your work a tone of authority. Convert dull, pompous passive voice and "businessese" phrases to active voice. For example:

Instead of	*Say*
"We are in receipt of"	"We received"
"Relative to"	"About"
"It has come to my attention"	"I recently discovered"

Instead of	*Say*
"It is the opinion of"	"I [we] believe"
"On the occasion of"	"When [During/On]"
"In view of the fact that"	"Since [Because]"
"In the event that"	"If"

Once you've edited the piece a couple of times, read it aloud. Try to hear it through the ears of your recipient, and listen for rhythm, clarity, and overall quality. Don't feel obliged to make your work sound like a memo or report. If you do, you'll become a literary mortician who may present the subject adequately but fails to bring it to life.

Pay strict attention to fundamentals of spelling, grammar, sentence construction, and proper word usage. Sound-alike words can turn a serious memo into a belly laugh; one manager recommended purchasing a vehicle with a heavy-duty "wench" on the front; another expressed concern about employees' "moral" problems.

Impress Your Receiver

Because we write to impress as well as inform, think about what makes your receiver tick. For example, if your boss is impressed by charts, graphs, footnotes, references, statistics, or other "gingerbread," plan your report accordingly. This isn't to say you should do a snow job—only that you must acknowledge your receiver's likes and dislikes, prejudices, and priorities if you want to make the best possible impression.

> **How well we communicate is determined not by how well we say things, but by how well we are understood.**
>
> **—ANDREW S. GROVE**

Proofread, Proofread, and Proofread!

Assume that every draft has at least one error that you haven't discovered. Computerized spelling checkers can help, but they check only for misspelled words, not for sense. One manager sent out hundreds of copies of a form letter that began, "In these days of educational buzzards . . . ." His secretary heard the dictated word *buzzwords* as *buzzards,* and the spelling checker gave it a clean bill of health. Neither of them proofed the letter and caught this mistake. A stock-room supervisor reported that the office supplies inventory included an oversupply of "onions kin" paper; boating regulations posted at one Orlando, Florida, launch ramp prohibit passengers from riding on a boat's "gun whale."

Give Helpful Examples

Examples can be life rafts. When you give clear examples, you've provided portable models that help readers comprehend your meaning. Examples that live in readers' minds help them reconstruct your ideas or concepts for themselves.

Provide Closure

If your memo or report requires a response, don't leave the recipient in limbo. Assign responsibility, request action, set a deadline, or provide a timetable for follow-up. Ask the question, "What should happen next?" and answer it so that your reader can take action without more information from you.

REVIEW AND REFLECT

True/False and Multiple Choice

Answer the true/false statements by placing a "T" or "F" in the space provided. Answer the multiple-choice questions by circling the number of the best answer.

a. ____ It's usually best to write a message when you want immediate feedback.

b. ____ Information should be written instead of spoken if several people must act on it.

c. ____ The communication barrier of inference-observation confusion applies only to what you see.

d. ____ Indiscrimination is a communication barrier that emphasizes differences and overlooks similarities.

e. ____ Polarization is reflected in the ultimatum, "Love me or leave me."

f. ____ Differences in status tend to discourage employees from communicating clearly with their managers.

g. You should usually speak instead of write when:
   1. You want immediate feedback.
   2. Several people must follow the same directions.
   3. Subordinates are likely to forget or ignore your instructions.
   4. You want to take a firm position on an issue.

h. After meeting Dr. Flanagan at a party, you ask her opinion about a pain in your back. She answers, "I'm a veterinarian." This experience illustrates the communication barrier of:
   1. Allness
   2. Frozen evaluation
   3. Inference-observation confusion
   4. Status or position

i. The speaker who says, "I've told you everything that's important about how to do this job," is guilty of the communication barrier of:
   1. Frozen evaluation
   2. Pointing and associating
   3. Allness
   4. Inference-observation confusion

j. The comment, "All cars are the same—four wheels and an engine," illustrates the communication barrier of:
   1. Indiscrimination
   2. Allness
   3. Pointing and associating
   4. None of the above

k. Which of the following comments illustrates the communication barrier of polarization?
1. "There are two sides to every story."
2. "If you don't agree with what I say, then you must disagree."
3. "We prefer to hire only people of German ancestry, because Germans are famous for their attention to detail."
4. "Only tell the boss what you think she wants to hear."

l. Which of the following statements illustrates the communication barrier of frozen evaluation?
1. "When Harriet was one of my students, her work was merely average. No doubt she's an average employee."
2. "I knew John four years ago, so I don't think my opinion of him would be valid today."
3. "People who excuse themselves accuse themselves."
4. "I may look busy, but I'm only confused."

m. Managers who are trying to improve their listening skills should:
1. Listen negatively and disagree with as much of what the speaker says as possible.
2. Criticize the speaker for not using techniques that the managers enjoy best.
3. Accept everything that's been said and assume it's all important.
4. Compare and contrast the speaker's remarks with their personal experience and other information.

n. _____ The amount of detail you provide with a directive should depend on the person with whom you're working.

o. _____ You should remind employees of your formal authority each time you give them a directive.

p. _____ Selecting three employees out of ten to take an inventory during a weekend would best be done by giving them a direct order.

Put It in Focus

a.   Rewrite the following memo clearly and concisely:

To: All present employees of the purchasing department

From: Vernon Verbose, Purchasing Department Manager

Subject: Waste materials

It has come to the attention of management that a frequent and inordinate expenditure of funds has been required to adequately maintain our duplicating apparatus. Our resources allocated for such work have been seriously depleted in an effort to maintain this equipment at an optimum level of efficiency and productivity for everyone concerned.

As a result of this situational exigency, management may have no alternative except to curtail all social and operational activities in or about said apparatus and to prohibit the operation of the coffee refreshment center in its present proximity and operational configuration.

In the event that such liquid refreshment and its accompanying social bonding cannot be matriculated without evidence of coffee-brewing by-products being inadvertently assimilated into the mechanism of said duplicating apparatus, we shall, speaking for the management team as a whole, have no alternative but to eliminate and discontinue altogether the existence of the coffee refreshment facility.

_____

_____

_____

_____

_____

b.   Rewrite the following phrases for clarity and sim-
     plicity:

     1. A check in the amount of $5 _____

     2. We have made a determina-
         tion that   _____

     3. Prior to receipt of your let-
         ter   _____

     4. At that point in time   _____

     5. At this point in time   _____

     6. I was present at this meet-
         ing in person   _____

     7. Enclosed please find   _____

     8. I have taken the liberty of
         enclosing   _____

     9. I'm taking this opportunity
         to reiterate   _____

     10. This office is not in a posi-
         tion to   _____

     11. Please be advised of our po-
         sition on the matter   _____

     12. This communication is in
         reference to   _____

     13. Please afford me the oppor-
         tunity   _____

     14. I would like to extend my
         personal invitation   _____

ANSWER KEY FOR REVIEW-AND-REFLECT ACTIVITIES

CHAPTER 2

Matching

a. 5, 8
b. 5, 8
c. 2
d. 7
e 1
f. 1
g. 3
h. 6
i. 4

CHAPTER 4

True/False and Multiple Choice

a. 1
b. F
c. T
d. 3
e. 3
f. 4

CHAPTER 5

True/False and Multiple Choice

a. F
b. T
c. T
d. F

e. F
f. T
g. T
h. F
i. T
j. F
k. F
l. 4
m. 2
n. 2

CHAPTER 6

True/False and Multiple Choice

a. F
b. F
c. F
d. F
e. F
f. 4
g. 3
h. 4
i. 1,
j. 3

CHAPTER 8

True/False and Multiple Choice

a. F
b. F
c. F
d. T

e. T
f. 3
g. 4
h. 4

r. F
s. T
t. T
u. F
v. 1
w. 4

CHAPTER 8

Put It in Focus

b. N
c. Y
d. Y
e. N
f. Y
g. N
h. N
i. N
j. Y
k. N
l. Y
m. Y
n. N
o. Y

CHAPTER 11

Put It in Focus

a. S
b. MA
c. S
d. C
e. MI
f. C
g. MA
h. C
i. S
j. MI
k. S
l. C
m. MI
n. MA
o. C

CHAPTER 11

True/False and Multiple Choice

a. T
b. F
c. T
d. 3
e. F
f. 4
g. T
h. F
i. 2
j. 1
k. F
l. T
m. 2
n. T
o. T
p. 4
q. F

CHAPTER 12

True/False and Multiple Choice

a. F
b. T
c. F
d. F
e. T
f. T
g. 1
h. 3
i. 3
j. 1
k. 2
l. 1
m. 4
n. T
o. F
p. F

CHAPTER 12

Put It in Focus

a.   To: Purchasing department employees

        From: Vernon Verbose, Purchasing Department Manager

        Subject: Coffee grounds in the copy machine

People keep spilling coffee grounds in the copy machine, and repair costs have gotten out of hand. If we don't move the coffee machine farther away from the copy machine, we'll have to cancel the coffee service.

Please suggest a new location for the coffee machine by Wednesday afternoon.

b.
1. A check for $5
2. We have decided
3. Before we got your letter
4. Then
5. Now
6. I attended this meeting
7. Here is
8. I have enclosed
9. I want to repeat
10. I/we cannot
11. Here's what we think
12. This letter/memo is about
13. Please give me the chance
14. I invite you to